I have been here before in many guises, always with
the intention of putting to rights the uncaring ways
of others for their Earth.

But as always, you of man have had to make your
own decision – whether to believe me or not.

In this book I tell you a little of those past times.
Some of you may even recall the action of them.
You would then understand my way.

The Stewarts,
525, Kingston Road,
Ewell,
Nr. Epsom,
Surrey.

28/4/79

WOULD YOU
BELIEVE AN ALIEN?

penned by
KEITH EDMUNDS

POWER PUBLISHING (U.K.) LTD.

First published in 1978 by Power Publishing (U.K.) Ltd
Brockwell Cottage, Sowerby Bridge, West Yorkshire
HX6 3PQ
Telephone Halifax (0422) 31013

Printed and bound in Great Britain by C. Nicholls
& Company Ltd, The Philips Park Press, Manchester

WOULD YOU BELIEVE AN ALIEN?

CHAPTER ONE

In a small city near to the place called Emsophor. It was thought that a child there was the new messiah, king of kings, leader of man. And it was proclaimed by many men and women of wisdom that it was so. Now this child was a young one and had come with its parents to visit relatives, but when the parents arrived they found that the authorities had commandeered all the accommodation, so that courtiers visiting a great pagan ceremony could bring all their servants and body-guards. Now all that remained was that they share the stable with their relatives and their horses. – Not a farmyard as farmyards are today, but little more than a shelter for horses.

The wise ones knew where the babe was, and spoke to all that came to the small city, telling them of its wonder. – How it shone – and indeed it did, but not with a noticeable radiance as you would expect, but it was so happy and showed it outwardly. Now Herod heard of this child and did not think of it as a menace in any way – until one, Simon, told him how so many that came to the city were kneeling at its side praying for deliverance from religion. This incensed Herod. You must realise that he considered that none should be knelt to, only him or the Gods.

Now Herod Agrippa was up to that time, a kind enough one – bringing custom to the priests in exchange for their teaching the people that he was a God. He travelled widely – all over the vast empire of Egypt which he ruled. And wherever he went his people marvelled at the great show of power and pageantry. His presence would be proclaimed throughout the neighbouring towns and villages, and many men and women would come to glorify and worship this so-called God on Earth. As he travelled from place to place, the Herod was accompanied by many priests and councellors – as well as a vast following of soldiers, body-guards, and servants – there were no Romans in those days. They only came to Egypt many, many years after the death of Agrippa, and they only infiltrated in a small way along the coast part near to what is now called Israel.

The visit by the Herod was particularly welcomed by the people of the area, because the crops that year had failed badly, and they needed the trade that would come from such a large gathering. The priests also welcomed the visit, because they could use the emotion brought out by the pomp and ceremony to encourage further worshipping of Ra. (Ra was the sun-god that most in those times worshipped). But they and their Gods could not make the crops grow any better.

The father of the young child – being a tradesman – hoped to profit from the gathering. But he had not realised the extent of the festival, and so was forced to dwell in a stable. The shelter was small and crampted – merely providing a cover from the elements. Like other shelters adjoining it, the stable looked out on to a open area, a courtyard – and it was here that the family stayed.

So when Herod Agrippa was told that his subjects were kneeling down to a small child – and a Jewish one at that – he was furious! Never in all his days as a Herod had he heard of such an insult, and what he thought of as a defiance of his authority. When his priests heard of the child, they also urged that Herod take action against such a bad influence. Ironic, is it not – that the ruler of such a vast Empire should be afraid of a small child.

It was the day before the large religious ceremony was to be held, and everyone was preparing for the forthcoming day. Business was brisk. Small stalls were everywhere as traders vied for the eye of the wealthy. The once small city had again become a hub of activity, and on this day a large crowd had gathered outside the courtyard, for news of the child had spread quickly throughout the city. The parents were surrounded by food and clothing, and a variety of other gifts – by now they themselves were anxious about the publicity that their presence was receiving – so they planned to leave the next day.

But they had already stayed too long. For as the crowd chatted in the mid-day heat, a loud noise was heard – then without warning, Herod and his men rode quickly into the gathering. Immediately there was chaos, and screams of fright burst forth from the crowd. Agrippa ordered his soldiers to surround the crowd, and many frail bodies were crushed or wounded by the soldiers horses, as they ploughed through the people. What followed was a massacre.

In an attempt to stop the people from escaping, Herod and his men drew blood. And more blood. And the more that the soldiers drew blood the more the crowd panicked in trying to escape death. Herod then started to enjoy the blood-bath, and once this happened – he showed no mercy. Few in that place were left alive at the end. The whole area outside the stable was strewn with the dead. Men, women and children. Such was religion that it killed and tortured the weak or the non believer.

But nowhere in the mass of bodies was there to be found the child and it's parents (even though the father had been hurt). They, together with others who had been standing near to a passageway, had managed to escape from the yard before the soldiers could manage to block off the exit. When Agrippa realised his failure, he was furious – so much so, that he took up his weapon and killed the soldier who by his slowness, had made possible the escape.

Thinking that the child and its parents would leave the city as soon as possible, Agrippa ordered an immediate search to be made of the surrounding country-side. A search that was to prove unsuccessful.

The pagan festival was held as planned, and memory of the

9

previous day's massacre was soon forgotten. Another massacre had been arranged for that day – one that was planned down to the smallest detail. This was the sacrificing of human slaves to the Gods. Most enjoyed the ceremony, and afterwards the people of the city wined and dined. But there was one who could not forget the massacre at the stable. That one was Herod Agrippa. For the memory of that day of slaughter plagued Agrippa for ever afterwards, and where once he had been a gentle one – loving of his family and people – he now became so cruel and uncaring.

But the child and its parents could not be found. For whilst the soldiers were searching outside the city, they remained within the city. And then, when the search was abandoned they quickly left that place. You see, the child had a task to fulfil upon this Earth, and it was not yet time for his life to be ended. This one was to show man a better way to live. He was to bring to man a great way of gentleness and caring – speaking words of wisdom and understanding of his Soul. He told man of man's own Soul. You know him well, his name was Jesus.

Man in those times was so callous. Human life was cheap – especially if the skin was of the darkest. Slaves from south of what is now Sudan were brought into Egypt to serve the wealthy or to be sacrified to the Gods. Even the natives of Egypt lived in fear of their lives. For it was that if a person was discovered to be going against the priests or their minions – then he or she could be imprisoned – murdered or even sacrificed at a moment's notice. Law and justice at that time merely depended on the local priests and counsellors of the Herod.

Understand that the empire of Egypt in those days was vast. No arid deserts as today. But already the deserts were commencing, and all over the empire crops were failing – each year the yield was less. Man grew his crops and took them from the soil, but failed to nurture the ground. So the soil, lacking in nourishment, failed in its task of providing.

Jesus was sent to warn man what would occur if he carried on with his stupid ways. He spoke out to man against the evil ways of religion. All too clearly he saw how its fear held the Egyptian people in bondage. He showed man the way of the priests – proving time and again that no Ra or other Gods existed. Warning man how the land would become useless desert if man did not nurture the soil as intended.

Jesus asked man to care – not only for himself and fellow men – but all the animals, birds and insects also. No matter how the other acted towards him, Jesus was always caring. All that mattered to Jesus was that man cared for his own Soul. He asked man to share instead of being selfish and greedy – just as he shared with all, just as he made others happy – so he shared the way of Soul.

*   *   *   *   *

Now I speak to you of a most important matter. I bring to your notice the way of God. *I* do not know this way, for in these lands of ours there is no such being to be found. Of that I can assure you. So let me try to enlighten you further.

Could it be that your Soul is the one that you refer to as God? Your Soul (the Soul of all mankind) made all that you are aware of – even yourselves. Yet you ignore your Soul and imagine that there is some other being taking care of you.

This being then must by-pass your Soul – but how can it? There is only your Soul linked to you. No other way possible. For if the link was severed, there is nothing left. Just as would be a hand cut from the body   it is no longer part of you, no longer living, soon it would shrivel and decay once again into the Earth from where it came. The link is your eternity. Your way of being a being.

Yet so many of mankind make a religion – in fact so many religions – from imagination. And the imaginings keep them from their true purpose for being on Earth. In fact the imagining of someone that you think you know of as God, has put fear and trepidation into the minds of many of mankind.

So many varied images does the word God conjure up in the minds of man. Is this mystical being a Demon, an Angelic like figure, an Idol, a King, a Pope, a subject of a book? Or is it just a name to which man applies qualities of his own imagination? Arrogant ones take over. They stand on boxes and say that there is "hell-fire", "devil", "god", "saints", and so on.

Ask them to prove their words and they are unable to do so in any way at all. Yet man believes their stories. It is these evil ones who sow the seeds of fear in the minds of man. Their weapon is fear – and they use it so well.

Man fools man into giving his material wealth – and talks him into ways of building churches, temples etc., to house those who, in return for his benevolence, lie to him! Who is fooling who? Time to take off your blindfolds, you who have covered your eyes and ears for too long. What about looking at all in a different way – in a better way – a caring way – a gentle way, a tolerant way? If you did so, you would recognise the perpetrators of religion for what they are – dealers in fear. Dealers in untruths. Dealers in evil. Dealers and wheelers – making rules and regulations that keep man from his Soul. Who is fooling who? Man requires a new way of looking at others in order to enable him to see who fools him.

You hear of so-called missionaries who go out to what are termed primitive peoples – peoples who are basically happy with a simple life. They are taught by the missionaries to want for more in greed, so they become unhappy and more discontented. The seed of fear is implanted in their minds – not only by such missionaries but also from witch doctors and voodoo leaders. These religionists cause doubts in many. Such doubts as whether or not one shall suffer in death and damnation, or suffer in other equally unpleasant and imaginary places. So, in fear, the primitive ones dare not take the chance – as they think. Dare not risk suffering at the hands of a god, or a spirit, or a demon. – Even at the hands of a god of love and mercy who is purported to massacre whole cities so cruelly and deliberately.

They say that their god requires this or that symbol to be worn or marked upon the body. The symbol could be a ring – whether it be on finger, through nose or through ear. It could be a tattoo on face or body. It could be a particular type of garment or head-dress. It may even extend to the mutilation of the child's organ or cocoon. And so it goes on. These religious ones infiltrate mankind, forcing those of their religion to go about advertising their particular brand name by a symbol – a label. Like branded cattle being led to the slaughter. Insidious is the only way to describe religion. For its ways pervade throughout all walks of life – suffocating the free choice of the individual.

Then there are other common-place and equally stupid rituals which are carried out within various religious build-ings. You have the follower expressing his misdemeanours to one who wearily sits nearby, and occasionally bursts forth with a few timely well formed phrases to suit the require-ments of his way of religion – such time-worn phrases they use. This pathetic ritual (combined with more grovelling and further parrot-like recitals of words and prayers) – this ritual is supposed to put all to rights without the follower having to change in any way whatsoever! Then there is the ritual where the convert is immersed in a pool of water. You do as much each bath night! There is the ritual in which bread and wine are eagerly imagined to be something that they are not. And so it goes on. Then you have the ceremony where a lump of substance is mourned after, yet those in mourning never realise that the thought, that was once this being, may well have already been born into a family in a nearby place – and even of a completely different faith! And so it goes on.

I speak out to you plainly of the insidious ways of the

religious ones, because for thousands upon thousands of years in time as man reckons, man has allowed himself to be shackled to these dealers of religious ways. They take man's very life on Earth away. They spoil the chance of man. These intolerant ones close the minds of man by their own intolerance, and by the fear which they instil. And how they instil! Right from the very start these liars indoctrinate man with their laws and subtle pressures – be it within the religious-based grouping that is the family, or within society itself.

Look hard and long at the men and women who dress in fine uniforms and read the words of a conglomeration of frustrated priests and scribes. Words such as heaven, hell, purgatory, death and damnation – words so meaningless – do these evil ones spout. Words which nevertheless instil fear into those who have been enmeshed into the net of religion. Fear, and respite from fear, being the ingredients of the lives of many such followers. Why do you think that these arrogant ones use such phrases as "the fear of god" and "god-fearing"? Such evil ones, these hypocrites. They look down upon their flocks in such a nice way .... and lie! And they know they lie!

I say to you of man, stand aloof from these arrogant ones. No longer go grovelling on hands and knees, bringing offerings to swell their pride and pockets. No longer be fooled by their shallow words and base rituals. Look carefully at these hypocrites who in fact condone killing. Yes, indeed, condone. Condone by such ways as blessing those who go out to kill others, and by their ways of eating the flesh of fellow beings – animals and birds.

They speak of an angry god. One who destroys men, women and children who do not pay homage. One from whom all must live in fear of retribution. Yet those who speak of such a one require maintaining by so-called lesser mortals, and require specialist training in the art of deception. So many of these religious ones drive weak and fearful ones into a state of crazed hysteria (and often suicide) by their threats, so-called exorcisms and excommunications, and other weapons of the mind. Such a callous and vicious lot are these. Occasionally, man manages to hear of some of these insidious and subversive activities of some religious ones. But those who are exposed are immediately dis-owned by religion as not having listened to the doctrines. – An easy "get-out" if ever there was one.

Associating with those of acceptable appearance and dis-associating with those of unacceptable appearance. – This is the way of religion – of god one minute, and of hell the next.

Ironic also, that the priests and religionists should mourn after those they *say* are supposed to have died and gone to a wondrous place. Even other priests (other "sure" bets) they mourn after! Then they rejoice at the birth of a person into this cruel world. Yet if the new-born came to this world from such a wondrous place, why rejoice at such an occurrence? Surely it would be more apt to regret the happening?

Religion *is* intolerance – purely and simply – intolerance. Intolerance of any who do not conform to its ways. Religion has turned man from his Soul – make no mistake on that score! Religion is like a virus or cancer on the Earth of man – always wanting more wealth and acclaim, and more power over the lives of man. Remember, the *first* god to be worshipped was greed!

No longer allow such ways to continue. No longer allow religion to warp the minds of man with fear. Take yourself away from these greedy ones, lest you also be pulled down by them as they fall. No longer walk in fear and humiliation. No longer kiss the ring and bow down in submission.

Soul realises that you cannot change all immediately – so you could consider the way I speak of a little at a time. Peace of mind comes with the way I guide you. You have your own wondrous Soul, allow it to guide and guard you through your life on Earth. Let it give to you the value that it has ready to unfold – the wonders of your Earth and the Universes. Listen, and discover your own purpose in life. What religion can give you the answer to that age old question – the purpose for life?

But how do I know if these words are Truth – you may ask? The answer is, you don't. Only by taking the trouble to consider and investigate for yourselves what is said, by listening to your thoughts and using the way that they point, looking at yourselves and all around with an open mind – only by doing this will you have your own proof. I do not ask you to believe what I say unquestioningly – it would be stupid to expect such a thing. Why should you believe what is said without your *own* proof? Too many nowadays follow along without question, like sheep. Too many are taken in by the sellers of untruths. Consider carefully what is said, with an open mind. Look. Seek Truth.

Understand that I speak out to you so that you may know, without doubt, what is truth and what is untruth. You have free choice to accept or reject what I point your way – all is free choice. But let me say that, when truth is sought after, then Soul puts all value, all caring towards man.

I speak out to you in Truth, for that is my way. Truth is so simple, so self-evident when you look it in the face. Truth is within each person's pattern of thought to understand and to use fully. Truth is a way of caring for mankind.

Truth is caring to say how you feel, to answer a question directly – confident in the knowledge that what you say is Truth. Truth is to use thoughts as they arrive – without twisting for self, for self-aggrandisement, for the false image of untruth, for convenience. It is to be open at all costs. To bare yourself for testing, for examination – to lay your cards on the table, so to speak. It is *not* to act a part that pleases or impresses, nor a part that "fits in" with what others around may think.

Care to be Truthful always – no matter what. Even admitting when in the wrong. Be one on whom others can rely for an honest opinion. One who will gently and firmly say how things are, not just how things appear. One who will speak out if something is wrong, and who will do all in his power to help others to understand themselves better. One who, when asked, will speak of another's good attributes as well as their faults.

Be one who is giving, ever giving, regardless of self – not one who says "yes" when the real answer is "no". Care to be Truthful, for by being Truthful you are indeed caring.

Many say that they look for Truth. But what they really mean is that they look for a way that suits them. They look to compliment themselves, as if they were perfect and knew everything already. If Truth was their way, then they would not be looking for it – and then they presumably would have found it!

Many live a lie. Many say what they do not mean and then try to cover up, to impress, to follow. So easy to be a follower in lies – expecially when so many around seem to get away with it. *Seem* to. But they do not. Not even one lie, large *or* small, is let slip by.

You notice how miserable a life can be as a result of lies, and more lies, and more lies. It eventually becomes such a headache, such a battle to keep the lies from unfolding. All pay, one way or another.

It takes courage to be Truthful – to lead in Truth amongst the followers of lies. It takes courage to be a leader – to pioneer the way of Truth on Earth.

Yet Truth is so good and wholesome. Truth is so important to peace of mind – so important to freedom. For Truth needs no explanation, no excuse. It is as it is. No cover up story is necessary.

By being truthful in all that you do, Soul will make the way easy – it will clear away all obstacles.

Now. Now is important. For now can be the start of Truth. Whatever has gone, has gone – that cannot be changed. But from now, you can determine to *be* Truth, whatever.

To live Truth. Now can be the start of caring – the start of Truth.

Man needs Truth. Will you have the courage to give it to him? Can you be Truthful – always – as Jesus was? Will you be a pioneer with those who come to lead man to Truth? You can be, for you are as I in Soul.

I now relay to you a story of such a pioneer. The story of a courageous one who sought after Truth.

*   *   *   *   *

He was an ordinary boy in many ways. Not bright, not dull. Not handsome, not ugly. His cloths were plain and his speech simple. On the surface he was just like any other teenage boy. Yet for all his high hopes and mischievousness, for all his impatience and worries, for all this, he was different. Very different.

For this young man cared for life – albeit mis-directed in many instances – but he tried. He tried in his own way – the only way that he knew how – to care. He cared, even when none cared for him.

Many times he would be used by so-called "friends" after he had taken each at their word. Many times he would be heart-broken when he discovered their true intentions. Yet there was an inner strength which carried him through all these disappointments. Even with all the deviousness around he knew that it was right to care and to give and to be gentle.

Oh yes, he resented being tricked and made sure that the same thing did not happen again. But in time he would forgive. For it was his nature to give anyone another chance to redeem themselves, no matter how they had acted in the past. He looked for the good in a person and gave the benefit of the doubt.

In his eyes, the peace the precision and the beauty of nature always demanded close attention – and he enjoyed so much, watching the birds and the animals as they played in careless abandon. But most of all he enjoyed the peace.

He loved children. It brought a smile to his face every time that he saw them happily playing together in their carefree way. In fact, the simplicity and directness of their way greatly affected his outlook on life. So much so that he irritated or embarrassed many friends and relations with persistent and searching questions. Because of this forthright manner many found his presence uncomfortable but very few had the courage to discuss this openly. Rather they would ridicule his simplicity when his back was turned.

But his strength was gentle. For many times he had the courage to walk away from violence or threats of violence. Yet he faced his fears. He would face all unknowns placed before him. And the reason? He was on a search – a search for Truth. He *had* to find Truth. He *had* to find a meaning – somewhere!

It was however, a quiet search – one within himself as much as in the world around him. He knew that if he discovered the way to find a meaning to life HIMSELF, then he could help others do the same. But the way? How to find the way? Because he had no answer to this question he was at odds with himself. For all around he saw the cruelty and selfishness of man but was at a loss to do anything about it –
Even though he wanted to help more than *anything else*.

He was born in a small village in the land of Judica some two thousand years ago. Judea being a part of this land that was, in those days called Judica. His family, like the majority at that time, was poor. Not poor as you know the word today, but poor in the sense that they were not of royal blood. They lived simply but adequately – none went without. His father was a brickmaker, his mother a seamstress. (Brickmakers in those days were akin to stone-masons of today).

Apart from helping his father for a few hours and doing jobs around the house, the majority of the day was spent enjoying the surrounding country-side or talking with friends and aquaintances. It was a good life in many ways.

But there was something that happened to this young man

that would dramatically change *his* life and the lives of many others. For one night, when he was not yet seventeen years of age, he had a dream. Not a dream, but a vision. A most wondrous vision – one in which he saw four things. A purpose, a face, a message and a name.

He knew his purpose in life. He knew where he came from and where he was going. He knew of his Soul. Not some intangible organ within the body, but his very consciousness, his higher self. He felt the gentleness and peace that it embodied and the great power and intelligence that was his true being – that was himself. He knew what had to be done.

Where there was turmoil and confusion Soul gave calmness and clarity. Where there was limit Soul gave no limit. Where there was darkness Soul gave light. Where there were questions Soul gave answers. He knew that Soul was life – both the giver and the taker – both the means and the end. For the first time he knew Truth. Absolute Truth.

Yet it was but a fleeting glance, for there was so much to see and understand. Too much to comprehend in such a short time. There were questions answered, but yet, more questions to be answered.

There was a face. A face that radiated gentleness. A face that he knew, yet he did not know. He knew this one like a brother, yet he had no brother! This one spoke gentleness. But a gentleness that was all knowing – a gentleness that was strength supreme. Then the voice spoke out to him saying, "leave all, and follow me". Leave all and follow me.

The face was gentleness and the name was Jesus.

This was the one that he knew he must seek out – there to find the answers to all his questions – there to find the light of life. Such was his task at that time – to find the one called Jesus, and learn more of the way of Soul.

He now had to find the way to meaning and to Truth.

I know. *I* was that young man.

Thus it was that I left my home and family.

A difficult task in many ways, for they were good people

and had given me much freedom to do with my life as I wished. I cared for them dearly, but *I cared for my task to help mankind even more*. They knew this, for they knew of my search. And so they prepared me for my journey as best they could – giving me the family horse, and a stock of carefully chosen provisions.

Many lands did I traverse, and many of man's ways did I see on my journey southwards. You must understand that things were not as they are nowadays in the lands that you call the middle east, and north and central Africa. Vegetation was lush – no deserts there then. All was vastly different to what you or your historians imagine it to be. Climate, geography, customs, dress, life-style – all were *so* different.

The Empire of Egypt in the times of Jesus covered such a large area, and was ruled by a Herod – a kind of a King as you term it today. It was wealthy, not only in jewels and precious metals – but also in trade, learning, perfumes, spices and cloths. From all over the world, traders came to barter for the exquisite oils and perfumes. There were also a great variety of spices produced here for in those days they were highly thought of, and widely used.

The finest of cloth (of which there is now no trace) was woven. Silks, cottons, wools and many more. Many of the cloths and garments would put todays manufacturers to shame.

Fruits, herbs, vegetables and grasses all grew in abundance. Vegetation thrived in the warm climes – even in the places that are now the Sahara and Saudi Arabia. Fine rich grass lands extended over much of the plains and valleys. What man has now spoiled, used to be a place of plenty. Indeed, in the early days of Egypt it was a good place in which to live in many ways, for there was much goodness in the way of man, as well as in the land around. But as always, man with his greed spoiled – spoiled himself as well as his land.

In the time of Jesus – when the Herod Agrippa was in power – the empire encompassed the lands which are now

Lebanan, Syria, Israel, Jordon, Saudi Arabia, Egypt, Lybia (in part), Sudan, Ethiopia and many others. The various principalities – or Kingdoms – within the empire, each gave allegiance to the Herod. His various children, relatives, or – occasionally – close friends would then be allotted to govern particular principalities, whilst he was elsewhere (as was more often than not, the case). Each battled for favour in his eyes. Depending upon the area that you were allotted, then it could be a blessing or a torment.

As I have said, I was born in Judica – what you now call the land of the Jews. Ah yes, the Jews.

They are originally Egyptians.

Before the era, or civilisation of Egypt, all the Jews, Egyptians, Persians and Arabians were from another continent – not Atlantis as many would have you think, but from a Southern land. Not as Africa is today with races of people of a colour that you call black, but from a land now under the ocean which adjoined the so-called southern Arab states.

The Jews idolised one called Abraham who was supposed to have spoken with God. This is but a fairy story! For the true ones who started the religion of the Jews were a group of *Egyptian* sacrificial priests. These religious fanatics were of the time before Herod the Great, so-called. They were at one time attached to his father's court but fell into disfavour.

So they ran away and hid for years.

Then they gradually came forward and formed a cult which they called after the land named Judica. At first they were not known as the Jews, but as Judicians (or, that is as near as your language allows me to put it to you).

This God that they now call Abraham, was not in the old times called or spelled in this way. Rather it was called Braham, after the cult now in India.

They loved sacrifice. And even today they mutilate each male child's body – as a mark of sacrificial splendour – to this God that they now call Abraham. Let it be known to all, that each time a Rabbi takes up a knife to a person in sacrifice in this day and age, he perpetrates evil. Evil, not only to the male child – but he also accumulates evil within himself, and pays dearly, oh so dearly, on the return to the transit realms of Soul.

Thus it is that in the middle east today, brother kills brother.

But it takes two sides to make a fight, for even the religion of the Egyptians is as bad. Those who take up this way are called upon to pay homage to the one called Allah, many times in the course of the day. This alone, blocks them from their Soul, not withstanding all the other evil ways that abound. Is one side of the coin then any better than the other?

But southwards I travelled, through Egypt and along the Nile – journeying on horseback, on foot or by boat. For the Nile was in those times a great trading route between Alexandria and the lands of the Mediterranean in the north, and Gaus – the centre of the government – in the south.

It was on my journey to find Jesus that I came upon a small community, which was near to the place called Thremes – or Thebes as you know of it nowadays. It was there that I first received my first ugly taste of religion.

This was such a religious place. It was the custom to make sacrifices to their so-called God – sacrifices of food, animals, and even man. The name of Jesus was blasphemy in these parts. I was soon to discover the *full* meaning of this myself.

On the surface, the people of this village seemed very amicable. But deep down they seethed intolerance, and hatred of any who did not worship as they.

I arrived at this place around mid-day and was made welcome into a small household where the family kindly offered me food and a place to rest for the night. At first they were very friendly and warm towards me – as any "decent, god-fearing" family would be in those parts. But after talking with the parents duing the afternoon and telling them of my purpose to find the one called Jesus, they were shocked.

They thought me evil and a blasphemer yet they said nothing. Even whilst I was talking, their thoughts turned to the great prestige that they would gain if they brought a follower of Jesus for sacrifice.

So, during the hours of dusk – when I was resting after my many days of travel – the parents, together with another, plotted my downfall. But whilst they arranged the purchase of a drug to put in my evening meal, my Soul warned me of their plan – in the form of a dream. A dream in which I saw myself, limp and unconscious, being carried by three pairs of hands to another place – then locked in a small room. I saw myself later shouting and struggling as I was dragged from this room to an altar – there to be killed as sacrifice to their God. Food. That was the key. I knew I must not eat *that* night.

Thus it was that later that evening the mother affably brought in some bowls of gruel. Of these five bowls, one had been drugged – this one they offered to me. But I politely refused, saying that I was very tired from my journey and wished to have a good night's rest. They thought that they would see me next morning. But I was gone before sunrise.

Southwards I travelled. Journeying through what you now call Aswan and "the Valley of the Kings", although in truth the statues were not of Kings. They were built long before the times of Jesus and long before the time of the one whose remains you take to be Tutankahmun. The remains are, in fact, of one who was born after the time of Jesus. – One who was a grandchild of Herod Agrippa.

Aswan, in those days, was a hive of activity. – A centre of trade and commerce. It was a major staging post for travel up and down the Nile. It was a second city to Gaus in the south.

It was also a centre of religion. A religion which worshipped many Gods, but primarily the God Ra – the Sun God. This was the one favoured by the Herod (Agrippa) at that time. And as the Herod was looked upon by most as a God himself, then Ra was the one in fashion. Very much in fashion! This worshipping of Ra was practised fervently in most parts of the land ruled by the Herod.

Because his rule was a religious one as much as a military one, the Herod's counsellors (if you could term them as such) were sacrificial priests. Each of these was well versed not only in the ways of sacrifices, ceremony and the Gods, but also of political and military strategy. They were a cruel and devious lot! Many used their power and position to kill or sacrifice those that fell out of favour. Life meant nothing to them. In a way, they were no more priests than are the religious butchers, judges or military advisors of today.

It was after many months of hard travel that I reached the outskirts of Gaus in the now Sudan. I had travelled over many hundreds of your miles. Yet throughout the journey my Soul had guided and guarded me. I had seen many cruel ways of man. But because of my effort, Soul had unfolded much understanding and given great comfort. I had left my parents – but I was home – if home be peace of mind. I had done what many older and more experienced men would not even attempt. To me, my journey was proof enough that with Soul, all is possible.

I shall never forget that day at Gaus, Gaus the city of magnificent palaces, courts and fine buildings. Gaus the city of cities where splendour and finery were common-place. Gaus the city of the Herod. Yet Gaus was nothing to me. No bricks and mortar were what I sought.

I sensed something very different about that day. It was hot and sunny – but that was not unusual in those parts. No. It was more than that. It was within me. A sense of excitement, a sense of great anticipation.

We met in a small clearing on a hill overlooking the city. He faced away from me and was talking to a group of eight others. Their gaze was fixed upon him as they sat on the rocks and ground round about. I knew it was he by the way his voice flowed on the warm air. As I approached nearer he stopped speaking and turned. I saw him. I saw Jesus.

I ran towards his open arms, tears rolling down my cheeks, clothes and body filthy with my journey. But it didn't matter. Nothing mattered now. Nothing mattered save being with my friend. My friend, Jesus. I was *so* happy. So very happy. Nothing would ever part us. Nothing! I *knew* that. There we stood – arms embracing each other and tears in our eyes. Words cannot describe how I felt. We said nothing for there was nothing to say. Nothing needed, for we knew what was in our hearts.

Like the few that were with him, I too, stayed to listen. Listen to the words of Soul which he spoke. I listened and learned. Learned much of value, then gave of that value to others. I walked at his side as he taught man of his Soul. We spoke out against religion, he and I. We spoke out against the selfishness and cruelty of man.

We spoke of tolerance, respect and gentleness.

We spoke of Soul.

My name?

My name was – Matthew.

CHAPTER TWO

I now bring to your notice the way of a Soulpart by speaking out firstly of the *very first Soulpart* to exist in the Lands of Soul. A Soulpart by the very way of the word, is created of a Soul. But there has to be a beginning – a way that a part of the Power and Intelligence of the Mass could evolve as a being in its own right. So I set aside a sector of myself – which I term for convenience, the Soulmaker – for the purpose of starting and maintaining the way of being that I term Soul. Only through this sector of myself – this Soulmaker – can Soul exist.

The Soulmaker was not in itself a being – merely an extension of myself, as is the mechanism for the pumping of blood in the body of man. Here the heart is not the *whole* body – merely a part of it allocated to perform a certain task.

Nor is the heart a being.

You may be could better liken the Soulmaker to the part of a female which is specially designed for the growth of the child whilst in the body.

So it was that I set aside a sector of Power and Intelligence for the growth and nourishment of my beings. The sector was well set out with all that would be required for the comfort and evolving of the beings.

Now you must realise that to evolve in Power and Intelligence for self (or "grow up" in a way) is all well and good, but anything which just grows and grows, creating more and more of itself, without purpose, is useless. So I arranged that each being would have a simple, easy, but necessary task to perform. A task which it must perform in order for it to grow up, so to speak (to grow up in the way that I use the phrase is to increase in Power and Intelligence). I arranged

27

that through the Soulmaker all the understanding of many, many ways – all the Intelligence of the Mass – would be made available to the new way of being, Soul. But only when the right to understanding – to Intelligence – had been earned.

The task which I set all beings within myself was to convert the dross of the substance in the lands of the Core, to a way of substance that could be used with Intelligence. To convert the hard, compact and unyielding substance of the land, into a way of substance so light and pliable. (Compare it if you will with the changing of a solid type substance on your Earth, to that of a gas type substance). The light and pliable substance is Power – Power necessary for all in Soul to exist.

By the new "being" performing this task it contributes not only to its own well-being (as a being of Power and Intelligence), it also contributes to the continuation of the Core of Power – of which it of course is a part.

I provide through the Soulmaker, the means of placing the dross for conversion. The being merely has to perform this conversion, or chewing over of the dross, whilst it is evolving for self.

You may imagine that what I speak of is as science fiction and not to be taken seriously. Yet what I speak of is truth. Truth of how all was and how all is in the Lands of Soul. You who read these words do so by your own free choice and I would never force you to do otherwise. Indeed, you have free choice to lay down this book at any time – even throw it on the rubbish pile if you so wish, but let me say to those of you who seek truth, that if you are patient with me all will unfold. And you courageous ones will know the purpose of this Universe and the way of man upon this Earth. Read on, or dismiss as rubbish, you have free choice.

Eons of time ago – measured in millions upon millions of your years – I created my first Soulpart. I placed a small blob of Power and Intelligence within the sector of myself set apart for the way of Soul. A Universe had been prepared for it and in this Universe there was an Earth.

Just as with the cell placed within the womb of a female before birth with all that is required for good healthy growth, so the first Soulpart was placed within the area of myself arranged specially for beings in their own right (children in a way). But unlike the unborn child in the womb, the beings within the Soulmaker would *live* as well as grow in Power and Intelligence. I wrap my cloak of strength and understanding around you all, constantly. And so it was with the first Soulpart.

The Universe or section of substance that was set out by the Soulmaker, was in all ways profitable to the Mass, it provided a way for the beings to work for it. It is the Power house of Soul. The set out of this sector of Soul was in all ways suitable for harmony. Harmony with my way, harmony with the ways of other beings, and harmony between the beings themselves, in fact, harmony in all ways.

It was arranged that on the Earth would be placed the dross of the substance that required to be chewed. But the dross was made so as to be pleasing to sense and use. – In a way, so that not even the beings were aware of the fact that it was dross.

For this to be done, it was necessary for the Soulpart to have at first a limited knowledge of the area of the Soul which contained processed dross or Power. Realise that this limitation must be so because otherwise the stay upon the Earth would be unbearable. And the change would be so great.

It would be like working in harsh conditions in order to maintain a comfortable living within the home. Without working in relative discomfort, no way could be earned to give comfort.

So the way of this Universe was arranged – out of necessity – to be made of dross, and the first ever Soulpart was placed upon it.

The entry on to the Earth was so gradual, and so gentle. Not like being thrust into something without prior warning or without a gentle acclimatisation so to speak. The way of the Soulpart on the Earth was brought into awareness gently, ever so gently. It came as one unknowing, yet one who knew that there was someone who would guide it and teach it in all ways. The contact with the Soulmaker was sure and clear and crisp. *That* was made sure of. Like a child|comes into this world the way it is – even with all the selfishness abounding. If allowed, the child grows and becomes in tune with the contact with its own Soul, with its creator.

The start was gradual, and the Soulmaker gave and gave to the first Soulpart. Giving, so that the being on Earth would never feel separated or lonely or uncared for. I gave constantly to this one, as I do to all beings, guiding them and gentling them along the way.

Through the Soulmaker I gave many examples to the Soulpart. Showing how things would be if this way or that way was taken. Putting to it the ways of understanding that I had previously come to know. By example I taught. I put a sense, then gently showed the Soulparts why it was, how it was, – what caused it to come into being – what ways caused it to diminish. I showed it ways of value – ways which gave purpose and understanding and caring. And I showed it ways of rubbish – ways useless to anything or anyone, ways which confuse and distort truth and reality.

Slowly but surely the young one learned about the one who created it, and by doing so, understood the best ways to use the Power which it earned. For all during its stay upon Earth it created Power for me and for itself.

It is now necessary to explain to you the way in which this conversion of dross substance to Power occurred.

It was not as you may imagine – a matter of sweat of the brow, or concentration of the mind. No need for such useless ways – not in this nor any Universe, any part of the Mass that is I. The Soulpart whilst on Earth had about itself a form. Not as you of man at present, but of a more clumsy nature. The form was in the way of a machine. I arranged that this machine would be kept in good order provided that it was used for the correct purpose. And that purpose being the conversion of dross to Power.

The Earth was necessary in order that the dross to be converted could be collected together in one place. It also provided a further function and that was the way of purifying the Output from the machine. Through the action of the Earth upon the Output, the dross substance would be made so fine, so light. You could compare the action of the machine and the actions of the Earth with a two stage process that you have on your Earth. The way of the machine carrying out the first stage in drastically changing substance, then the Earth finishing it off.

Such was the way things were with the first Soulpart to be placed upon an Earth.

The way of being evolved satisfactorily and Power was produced by the machine which it occupied.

Many other beings – Soulparts – I placed upon the Earth, and they too evolved and enjoyed their task upon the Earth. The way of Power began to flow to the Core through the Soulmaker, and I in return, gave all that was necessary for more Soulparts to be created.

I return now to the first Soulpart. It fulfilled the task upon the Earth, it had successfully completed the first part – the first step – on the way to understanding all that there was to understand. Whilst on the Earth, the way of understanding had been limited. (Necessary to do this, in order for the Soulparts to *earn* the right to evolve). *All* must be earned. You could compare it with a person being taken out of their natural way – free in all ways, and all seeing – and put in an unnatural or strange place with limited senses and freedom.

After having left the Earth however, this Soulpart was in a far differing way. It had, through the correct use of the machine on Earth, earned the right to enter a special section within the Soulmaker. This section I call the true realms of Soul.

Here, in the comfort and warmth of the true realms, the Soulpart started to *really* understand.

After a short time so much understanding had been gained that the Soulpart was asked to start on a new way for itself. This it gladly agreed to do. The new way was as a Soul. No longer a Soul*part* but a Soul. And so the Soulmaker gave the Soulpart a certain Essence of myself. An Essence which gave the part the ability to create new beings of itself. To this Soulpart I also gave much Power for it to start off its way as a Soul. Enough Power for it to create within itself:— a Universe, and an Earth, and parts of itself upon that Earth. Parts which would earn the necessary Power for Soul and the Core to continue in a good way. Parts which would be beings in a form arranged by the new Soul.

That was the way all happened at the start of the way I call Soul. I speak out to you of this beginning and of the happenings previously in order that you may understand yourselves better. You see, all that I speak to you of is for your benefit. I do not say do this, or do that, without first giving very good reason. Nor would I ask you to believe me without questioning further – without proving to your satisfaction that my words are Truth. For they *are* Truth. They are a Truth never before put to man in such a way of strength and caring. I say that you have free choice whether or not to care to find Truth, and whether or not you care to find proof of what I say.

All that I speak to you is Truth – plain and simple. I do not please, nor do I condemn. I merely state how things were, how things are, and how they can be. All is practical. All can be applied to the way of life of each upon this Earth at present. I now point out to you the way of Soulparts on this Earth of yours.

You are Soulparts. Parts of a mighty Soul which cares for you so dearly, even now. For even now your Soul gives you free choice. Free choice to change your way, free choice to ignore the words of Soul, free choice to be free in all ways. It cares. It cares greatly, and would never interfere with your decision.

You of man are on an Earth to do a task for your Soul – and for all of Soul. And remember, you are part of the one that created you. You are part of your own Soul.

The task of each of man is two-fold.

It is to evolve for self in Power and Intelligence, and it is to use the machine which you occupy to produce Power for Soul.

I will now explain further so that you can be clear of the way to go forward – that is if you care to do so.

You receive all understanding, all sensing and awareness, all by your own thoughts. No others' thoughts – only by your own. There is nothing that you or any can do upon this Earth without a thought.

You may well imagine that this is not so, or that you can even make your own thoughts. But can you? If you can make your own thoughts then how do you do this? How do you *then* make the thought to make the thought .... and so on. Also, why do you forget? And why can you not find an easy way out of difficulties?

I say that you do not make your own thought. You are merely a receiver of thought sent from elsewhere. And that elsewhere, is the Intelligence of this Universe – your own Soul. It is by the correct use of your own thoughts that you evolve for self, and allow others also to evolve for themselves. Your Soul sends to you two tracks or types of thought.

You come out of the darkness of slumber into the way of this Earth. You dream many dreams – some good, some not so good. Some dreams you recall, but most you are unaware of. For your dreams are really glimpses into reality – into what I shall call the transit realms of your own Soul.

In such glimpses you may view many wonders of your own Soul, recall a small fraction of the planned way ahead, or you could act out a lesson to guide the part of yourself upon Earth to a better way of being.

You must understand that dreams are not as you imagine – not imagination. They are glimpses of yourself, by yourself, and for yourself. That is, glimpses of your true being – your true self in Soul – and acted out *by* self for the thought of self in the body of man.

Man's life on Earth is like a play, where the stage has been set and the play well rehearsed. The curtain rises and the actors come on stage, living the parts that they have chosen to play.

Only during the short intervals off stage, do the players rest and be who they really are.

Dreams are as recollections of these intervals between the scenes – the short periods where reality comes to the notice of the actor.

In slumbers you go from the way of man into being. The thought that is you is taken back into your true being, with only a duplicate thought keeping the body mechanism "ticking over" so to speak. Once back in this state (in the transit realms), you perform various tasks in preparation for the following day, then relax and enjoy the peace of Soul. For these realms are places of great comfort – comfort far out-weighing anything that you know of on Earth, so peaceful and calming are they. But even these transit realms are as nothing to the true realms of Soul.

It is in the transit realms that the various ways of thought are arranged for the being on Earth. Whether it be planning the life before coming to the Earth, or whether it be living through *all* the following day's pathways during the hours of slumber. You see, all that man does has been lived through by him the night previously. – All the ways that he could choose to take – all possibilities. And depending upon the choice made whilst on Earth, so the part on Earth lives out a particular way.

As man is at present – not satisfied with one particular way for more than a short time – he in Soul puts himself to more work by having to provide and live through a multitude of ways. This is so vital in order that the part on Earth has free choice in the ways it wishes to take. For it is your Soul's way to allow free choice in all matters, and on no account will it interfere with or lessen that free choice.

Before commencing upon the task of creating new beings of itself – new Soulparts, the Soul of this Universe decided on a plan. A plan that would best suit its Soulparts and give them all the possible ways that the plan could go. The Soul then placed parts of itself – in form of man – upon the Earth. The plan was such that it provided these Soulparts with many varying ways of thought. According to the choice of thought, the Soulpart could evolve to become a being of great wisdom and strength – as was the Soul which created it.

The ways of thought were arranged to be of two types – those of value and those of rubbish (or lesser value).

The first type were the ways of understanding – the gentle ones tempered with the Intelligence of Soul – the ones which embodied the ideals of the Soul. These value ways would be so clear, comforting and sustaining to the part on Earth. If value ways were chosen, then they would bring the Soulpart great understanding of its own Soul, understanding of its own Earth and Universe, and understanding of exactly who and what it was. For one taking these ways, the way of life on Earth would be one of purpose, happiness and peace of mind.

The second type of thought were the ways of rubbish – those of non-understanding – those opposite to Soul in every way – the ones of untempered brute force. These rubbish ways would lack intelligence and so be destructive, confusing and unsatisfying. When these ways of rubbish were taken by the Soulpart on Earth, the Soul would arrange for them to be accompanied with such feelings as unhappiness and loneliness – done so that they could be clearly identified as being rubbish.

The Soul also gave man the facility to twist the thoughts which he received. Twist so that value could be received but then turned for selfish ends, causing it to become rubbish. It also gave man the ability to twist thoughts even further – twisting the rubbish ways to ways so vicious and so cruel.

In the present civilisation of man, the ways of value are those of caring, gentleness, respect, tolerance and non-encroachment. Ways of rubbish are those such as resentment, intolerance, selfishness, uncaring, emotion and judging.

These and many more ways are put by Soul so that you can choose which ones you wish to use. Value or rubbish – you have the choice. Ways of being depend upon you personally. You can adore such a way of Soul that all around you is rubbish. Now I tell you a story – a story of a way of rubbish.

In a time back in your history a man on Earth heard his Soul. He cared for what he heard for it told him of things to come, and how he could help man in a better way of understanding. He listened, and recorded what he heard. Then after arranging ways that could only benefit him materially, he spoke of the things to come.

The end of the world was predicted and many other items – how wars would come – and financial loss to many. He spoke of Kings and Consorts. So amazing were his predictions that he was invited to join the courts of that land.

Nostradamus they christened him amongst other titles. But many had cause to believe him. Many had cause to ridicule him. He is no more on Earth yet his legend lives on – but without understanding.

He could have been the means of putting to rights this Earth if he had listened without thought of self gain. As it was, his words were lost in the mass of untruths of others who also sought for self. Like so many of man at present, Nostradamus listened to his Soul in a way. But in a way of rubbish. He cared for his voice, but he cared for material more. And when rubbish is used understanding is withheld. So the words of Nostradamus were also without understanding – without the true caring that *is* a way of value.

Only by using value can you truly care for man, not by way of rubbish. By using value you receive all understanding and know for yourselves what is to be. You will then know that all that is intended to occur, will occur. You will know your own future. No use trying to predict with only the idea of self gain, for the information gained will be doubtful. Each one can know their own future merely by listening and following their voice within – the voice of themselves – the voice of their Soul.

Nostradamus tried to care, in a way, but it was not regardless of self – it was not value. Strength comes only with value, as does understanding. It is a strength of knowing, strength of being, a strength of purpose.

Nostradamus was unable to care for man and show him the way forward, because he lacked the understanding of how to do so. He chose to ignore the value – the understanding – of his Soul. Pity that one so great in the way of hearing Soul should have been so weak as to use it for self gain.

As part of a great Soul, Nostradamus was sent to this Earth to bring man understanding of his Soul. He was as you. He was of your own Soul, and it was his task to use the value of Soul. He heard the voice of Soul clearly – even through all the indoctrinations which his life as man had brought. He adored his voice so much, and knew it to be correct. He saw the value of Soul and he saw also the rubbish around.

But Nostradamus wanted the best of both worlds so to speak – best of Soul value and the wealth of man. He imagined that much of what he had already was value, when it was not.

He saw learning of his Soul as a giving up – when it was not. No, not at all. It was a replacing of the worries, troubles, and indoctrinations of man with something far, far better. His Soul only wanted him to be happy and peaceful, caring for man by caring for the voice within. – Just as it does for you now.

Nostradamus relinquished many vices and thought that he had given up much for Soul, but in reality he had only given up a few indoctrinations which were inconvenient to him. He saw rubbish as value, and so clung on to many ways that blocked off the value and understanding of Soul. By his love of things useless he failed in his task for mankind – for his fellow Soulparts – for his own Soul.

Now, many years later, your Soul has again arranged that words be put before man. Many words, in many forms. But this time they *are value*. In them is understanding. In them is the strength and caring of Soul. Your Soul holds out its arms to you, so that you may understand its ways and then care for all in a good way. I, Soul, say care for your own Soul first. That way you truly care for *all* other beings.

As in other plans which were implemented to bring man to a way of value, the attempt in the time of Nostradamus failed – not through lack of support, but through lack of a strong leader. You must understand that many from the highest realms of your own Soul and from the Souls close to the Ultimate, came with Nostradamus. Their task was to follow his example. But they had no example. They saw weakness instead of the strength that comes with Soul value. There have been many plans – before and after Nostradamus – but so often the one to lead is weakened by the trappings of self-gain. Nostradamus liked what *he* liked – just as did others around him.

The Courts in those times fascinated Nostradamus, for they had great power over the people, and provided him with the wealth he adored. After the prophecies which led to him joining the courts had been publicised, Nostradamus still contined to predict occurances in a way. You see, he was well aware of the ways of those in the courts and places of notoriety – seeing through the words and actions, noticing the small tell-tale signs which betray motive.

But he used the awareness that he had been given to pry into the intentions of those with power (to pay without them even noticing). It was by this method – by this milking of information – that Nostradamus furthered his way of prophesying. His predictions were useless but impressive, and served to maintain his elevated position in Society. Nostradamus was an expert fortune teller and confidence trickster, and as many today are, so was he – seeking self gain and prestige in his idea of life.

The part he played was the parts played in this day and age by so many who predict this and that. They hear a voice within and become afraid at first, for they do not know who speaks with them. So they talk to others who say that they hear voices also. Then each leads the other into believing that chinamen, or indians (red or otherwise) or bishops or nuns or children – spirits that have lived on this earth in ages before them – are invading their minds. Trying to take over their way of being.

Many use the method of self trance so that others will not condemn them if wrong information is given during this trance. What is trance as they call it? Some photograph those in trance and make a way of putting into the picture some distortion that can be identified as a shadowy being in the background.

Now it is not so – never has been so – that any spirit (by that you must understand that I use the word term of man) walks upon this Earth or above it, in any way at all. Those who in future perpetrate this idea will be shown their error by Soul. Dreams are lessons. Watch your dreams you who would fool others in future.

When man leaves this Earth plane he has no need or wish to come back to it in any other form. He then knows how all is in this Universe – knows how he was upon Earth and seeks to evolve.

Never do any return to this Earth in the form of ghosts, ghouls, spirits and so on. No such thing!

Man is on Earth to perform a task for his Soul – a task which requires a body or cocoon. Then, when the time allotted for the task is spent, the thought is withdrawn from the cocoon back into its true being. – A being uninterested in providing entertainment, fear or solace for those remaining. Especially when the ones on Earth have a wondrous Soul waiting to give all comfort to them.

Man on Earth has a body and a thought link to his Soul. Always this is the case. There are no exceptions. The thought comes to the receiving set or brain in two forms. These two forms I shall refer to as tracks of thought.

One track provides the thoughts necessary to maintain the body – to cause the heart to pump – the blood to circulate and so on. This duplicate thought track is sent to the cocoon during the whole time that the body is being used – day and night. And only when this duplicate thought is withdrawn can it be said that death occurs.

The other thought track – the original track – is one providing man with the many ways of Soul:– the seeing, speaking, hearing, sensing thoughts – the value and the rubbish ways of thought – the choice of which way to follow. In Essence, the original track is the one which man on Earth is consciously aware of. It is provided so that the being on Earth can evolve (which would not be the case if only the duplicate track was present).

Many times throughout the day the original thought causes an arm to move or an eyelid to blink. In these and many other such deliberate actions, the original track operates in conjunction with the duplicate – over-riding it in a way.

That in simple terms is the way man is on Earth. Thought. Thought sent to a cocoon. Not something floating about bodyless or formless. Not something invading other beings in any way. But the thought that is a Soulpart occupying one – and only one – cocoon.

As I have said previously, each of man return to transit realms during the hours of slumber. In this case the original thought link is temporarily withdrawn to transit realms. But the duplicate thought still remains, in order to keep the body functioning. When both tracks of thought are withdrawn (in death), the Soulpart goes either to the true realms of Soul – if the task on Earth has been fulfilled – or else it returns to the transit realms if the task was not completed in any way. It is in the transit realms that the Soulpart waits for another opportunity to fulfil the task in a further life upon Earth.

Man's thoughts are so vital to him. They are his link with his Intelligence – with his Soul. They are his lifeline.

So many thoughts you have – to run, jump, move around, to listen, to feel, – so many, so different, so wonderful.

Man could do so much more with his thoughts if he cared to do so. But even in the way of receiving thoughts, man hinders himself. Hinders the passage of thought through the channels to the brain, by not allowing a child to cry its fill at birth. Because of this, many bodily functions are impaired and instead of receiving the thoughts so clearly, they are dulled slightly. You could say that the crispness has been taken from them. Nevertheless they are there for all to hear – and hear quite easily.

By this mis-treatment early in life, passageways for thought remain partially blocked, and no amount of coughing and sneezing or surgery can completely clear them. Once the damage is done there is only one way that these passages can be completely cleared. And that way cannot be taken by any on this Earth. Your own Soul is the only one who can clear out the dross within. Your own Soul. But it will only do this when the right has been earned – when the Soulpart on Earth makes an attempt to listen to its Soul. I, Soul, promise you that this is so. I promise that if you truly listen to the voice within, then the voice will be made so clear. As clear as it was with Nostradamus.

Nostradamus was sent to clear the way for man. So your Soul took away the blockages in order that he could put to man what was put to him. But even with such clarity of thought he failed to do this, and the thoughts received were turned to self gain and deception. He failed to tell man of man's own voice, and how each can hear as clear as clear.

No need to rely on what others say. No need to go to so-called mediums, priests and the like for a message. No need to return ever again to this Earth. Each one on this Earth has their own contact. Each one can know for self. It costs nothing and is so simple to achieve. Merely listen – listen to the voice within. The voice of your own Soul.

Your Soul will give to any of its beings. It gives constantly what each being thinks it requires for self. Whether it be value or whether it be rubbish. If the being requires wishy-washy, selfish and emotional ways, then they are given.

If however, the being requires proof – requires a way of knowing how all is – requires happiness and peace of mind – then it is given. Over and over again it is given.

For those courageous ones who seek Truth, proof *will* be given – not by others at a price, but by your own Soul. You who seek Truth, look first to your own thoughts – to the voice within. For that is where you will find your proof – within your own thoughts. Thoughts are so valuable. They *are* your own Soul.

There are a few on Earth who already listen to their thoughts. But they do not listen long enough in caring – only wanting to give a message of some sort to any who will listen to them. They hear the voice within clearly, but do not understand how or why it is there – never realising that there is a task to perform for their Soul, (not only by themselves, but by all others also). They appear only to want self aggrandisement – prestige for self.

I would say to those who hear the voice within, that it is no good listening just for messages. Far better to seek to understand your own voice, so that having done this you can then pass on that understanding to others. Realise that it is for each one to understand their own purpose in life. That is where the caring comes in – the understanding of your purpose in life. No use trying to help others in messages or advice until you understand firstly your own task, and secondly the task of the other. So you see how foolish it is to behave as you do, when you could be working for the fulfilment of your own dear Soul.

There was in an age long gone such a man, who worked for the benefit of others of his own kind – Soul.

May I now allow you the pleasure of knowing that many saviours have been on Earth to assist you over the ages of this Earth. You may not at this stage believe my words, but I say, all is Truth. If you look deeply you will know it to be so.

This time was cruel. Man was so often blinded or maimed. The ruler, a vicious Queen, loved to see man tortured – it was fun and pleased her. This was two or so thousand years before the time of Jesus, but even then there was a saviour.

As all along the line there have been many attempts – many many failures, to convince man of his Soul.

*   *   *   *   *

The saviour in this life-time was not one who is remembered by man in any way – and yet he left his mark – for he took many along the way to Soul. Many Soulparts evolved to the high realms of Soul through this great saviour whose name was IVON.

*   *   *   *   *

I relate to you now an instance in this life when he was not yet twenty. But even at this age he was in a way of Soul. His name was Marcus and he went from place to place with such authority and grace of being, constant in his support of the one, Ivon.

He was entering the gates of a city – entering by a dusty road along which he had been travelling for many miles. At the left hand side of the stone pillars or gate posts, sat a cripple.

There he sat – all dirty, sunbaked and cross legged. In his hands was a wooden bowl. Marcus stopped when he heard this one cry out for alms, and walked over to him.

He was such a sorry sight – clothed in tatters – hair in filthy knots – eyes, an ugly mass of blood and puss. None cared for this one – not even the dogs which abounded throughout the city.

Yet within the ugly exterior was a kind heart. He was a dreamer, and many a beautiful story would he tell to those who gave money as they passed by. None knew the purpose or meaning of his dreams – not even he. Marcus looked down at this one as his crusty voice weakly asked for pity.

After a short pause, when he became aware of the young man's presence, he held out his bowl and continued his pleading. Even though Marcus said nothing, the cripple went on and on telling of his meagre requirements. Then slowly, as his repertoire dwindled, his speech became disjointed. He continued in this manner for a short while – speaking, as he thought of something else to say, then pausing, speaking, pausing. Suddenly his expression changed and he blurted out words of derision, telling Marcus to go on his way in order that he could benefit from more "generous" customers.

Marcus replied by putting to him a better way of being. But this the beggar dismissed as being impossible for a man in his condition. He spoke of his problems in a whining way, saying that the whole world had been cruel to him, and how he had been crippled and blinded through the cruelty of one he was so afraid of.

Marcus put to him the way of Soul – the way of the saviour at that time (he had heard a few stories of this one), telling him that this was an opportunity to help man – not as a cripple. An opportunity to help man – not just his few friends and acquaintances, but also his enemies. The beggar tentatively agreed to try this, if Marcus showed him what to do. So the strong one spoke out to him of the caring and gentle ways of Soul, and how by turning to his Soul, the beggar could *live his dreams*.

Then holding out his arms, Marcus asked him to choose.

44

To choose to stay in the way of man as a blind cripple, or to choose the way of Soul and enjoy peace and well being. He now had the chance to stand up and follow Soul.

Uncertain at first, he stretched out his arms to Marcus and grasped hold of his hands – his arms shook, then his whole body shook. He could feel his legs! He moved his legs – first one then the other – like a newly born foal. You would understand if you had felt his hands in yours as Marcus did, squeezing so hard. Slowly, ever so slowly at first, he rose. Up. Up. Up he came towards the sky which he faced, throwing his arms around the others shoulders, but Marcus gently took them from himself and stepped back.

There he was on his own two feet. Still shaking and rocking to and fro – but he stood. Oh yes, he stood alright! He cried out in such triumph and joy for he could walk. He *could* walk!

Marcus placed his hands over the ugly mass that was the eyes, and told him to look at the one who stood before him. For as Marcus took away his hands, the beggars eyes were no longer swollen and indistinguishable – merely blood-stained and watery. They walked through the gates to a water trough where the beggar washed away the blood and puss from his eyes and face.

He stood and looked (as did all those around). No sound did he make. Then his lips began to quiver, his mouth slowly opening in surprise. A light. A light. He could see a light.

Again he washed.
He could see the gate – and the horses – and the people around. He could see his hands!

He shook all over, then moved, then walked. First one step – then the next – then more – then more. He staggered about, walking to anything or anyone he saw. He was crying, yet he was laughing.

All was in an uproar. All around stopped and stared at this man who was a blind cripple just a few minutes ago. This man to whom they had given a coin or two over the last days, weeks, years. This man who was now walking about shouting with joy.

Yet he had fallen. He had fallen!

All around let out a cry of anguish. He had fallen, what will happen next?

But no. This is but of a moment. For he again moved. He again raised himself on two feet.

A smile came, then tears, then a look.

A look which means all. – A look that is a new born babe.

This man was born again.

Once again Marcus held out his arms to him. He walked to him.

He *walked* to him, and Marcus held him close in his arms.

No words.

No words necessary.

No words suitable.

Soul is All. – It so is.

CHAPTER THREE

Dear Scribe. Through you I relate a very unusual story. The words I give to you may sound strange, for you are used to my way, and not the way of another's Soul.

But this most wondrous Soul has no means of putting its words through the media of its own Soul sector. For this sector – not a bad one at heart (in fact, in his own way, caring greatly for the Ultimate) – this one, this sector, is so engulfed within the way of spiritualists, Palmistry (as it is called), the way that he works, that he has no time to try to understand the contact with his own great Soul.

He neglects his Soul for the dross of Man. He is of Our Lands but does not yet believe it. Later, he will know for sure. But these words of his Soul are intended to inform Man of other ways of life, in a vastly differing Universe to most others.

I say that it is now time for the story to unfold.

You must realise though, that this one has had *so many* visions – so many – so many thoughts from his Soul. He is, in a way, a gentle one – but afraid. For he has listened to the stupidity of religion – which he was brought up amongst – and later to spiritualists jargon. These have scared him stiff. Made him closed minded to his own wondrous Soul, and he takes a crumb here and there, when his Soul waits to give him the full loaf. – Just as Man.

It is a vastly different place – the place I speak of. This Universe has no Earth and it draws its Power from the Core of Power – The Ultimate. The beings are of all types – types from nearly every Universe. The Soul in control is a Wise One. – So caring of its unusual parts. I say its Soulparts, but in truth this Soul is not as others, for it has no Soulparts of itself. Preferring instead, to assist "lost"– shall I say – Soulparts of other Souls. This Soul cares greatly – cares so dearly for others different to itself in many ways, but yet Soul. It is like a foster-mother who takes it upon herself to care for, and teach, children who have chosen to turn away from the one that gave birth to them – the one who yet still cares for them.

The existence of this Universe shows, in part, both the oneness and great caring between both Soul and Soulparts, and between Souls themselves. It has been such a wondrous effort that it has made to *all* other Souls. For no Soul cares to destroy a Soulpart – even if the Soulpart repeatedly refuses to evolve. So this Wise and Mighty Soul took it upon itself to care for others unlike any in their own Soul – misplaced ones, I shall term them.

I first speak to you of this Universe for it is unlike any other and is, in a way, odd. I speak first of the set-out of this Universe for, as I have said, it differs greatly from all others.

It is not a Power house, but a place of strict learning. Thus it is arranged so that none who are sent here escape learning. Let that be understood. It is necessary to describe the Universe in order that you of man have an idea how all is, for many of your Earth have taken *themselves* to this place. This Universe caters for weak ones – Soulparts not able to face any task whatsoever.

Man at present calls them suicides.

But understand that all those *you class* as suicides are not all so. Some, through the fault of others, die taking tablets that dull the senses so that they know not what they do. *These* are not suicides. These have been blatantly inveigled, in many cases, into believing that the tablets are for their own good. So, when those who have prescribed them leave this Earth, *they* are classed in place of the suicides and sent to the Universe I now speak of. Soul repays when its Soulparts are too weak to repay themselves.

48

This Universe, like others, has many realms but there is no let-up, shall I put it, from teaching. The teaching is constant and necessary, for words as man uses them are not sufficient when teaching those who are afraid.

In these realms, the beginner from another Soul is first acclimatised – invited into a kind of group where others, as he or she, have perpetrated a certain deed or several differing misdeeds.

Then, after a short period, they are made to go over and over the misdeed until they cry, enough. Some realise quickly the error of their last life upon an Earth. With others it takes so much longer.

Once the folly of their ways is completely understood, then this Wise Soul takes them into another group where they meet other beings differing from them – not in colour alone – but in shapes, sizes, etc. For each Soulpart has about it, the same form as from its original Soul. There they have to learn tolerance and patience each with the other. And when eventually the group as a whole – and it MUST be as a whole – can live together in harmony, they then go to another realm where there are again different beings. Of these beings some are gruesome in shape, others gentler, but again all must learn to live together in harmony.

Each step, or stage of learning is, in a way, a gradual but continual one, for each Soulpart is given only what he or she is capable of overcoming. No steps are left out, no aspects of tolerance, gentleness and respect let go by. The learning is thorough. Very thorough. But never-the-less gradual and surmountable. As each stage is overcome and each realm of this particular Universe traversed, then eventually – over the course of time – they can reach this wondrous Soul.

Once there they can rest and enjoy. Many choose to stay, liking their new home – their new Soul. But others care to evolve even further, so ask to be allocated a task. This Wise Soul agrees and sends them invariably, to a Universe that is

49

requiring assistance. Not as mankind requires assistance. In Soul we each assist in varying ways.

If the Soulpart performs the allotted task in a satisfactory way then, on return, it is offered a way out of its problems. It can return to the Earth of its own Universe and repay to others. But it can never, never – I repeat never – rejoin its original Soul. It stays linked to the Wise One.

It has occurred many times that the Wise One has recommended one or two here and there from its Universe to go forward and become Souls in their own right. And excellent Souls they have made. So you see, even these ones – these ones who were so weak and fearful – even they, through the care and understanding of Soul, can eventually be strong.

The Wise One watches and waits. For none – not one – progress without earning in the realms of this Mighty Universe of Odd Beings.

I take you now to a particular part of this Universe – the receiving sector where Soulparts come into Soul. It is a sad sector, for it is here that they take their leave of their own Wondrous Soul, and know that never again can they contact. Even when a task is set and they return to repay on the Earth of their original Universe – even then, they have no contact with their own original Soul. It is such a sad time – both for the original Soul and the Soulpart when the link is severed. But severed it is. For Souls cannot go forward with such weak links attached. So instead of folding the Soulparts out of existence – out of eternity – they are given a chance to redeem themselves in this special Universe.

The Wise One is gentle, kind, considerate to all who enter its Universe – but is firm, and does not judge them. It shows them by example, the error of their ways.

Such a Wise One, this Soul.

Your way dear scribe of writing for another has still a way to go, for I relate to you other ways that have occurred – especially upon this Earth that you now reside upon.

Others have much to say also, and you can be their voice.

Nothing shall be left out of the way of giving for the benefit of man.

Write on dear scribe.

*   *   *   *   *

I relate to you a story – only in part, for I refrain from speaking fully. In this Earth, at one period, dwelt an evil one. Not in the way of religion, but in the way of evil of thought. The time was not long gone. It was in the lifetime of many of you of this age. But such a one existed and you know of him. His deeds were so foul that never again was he to be allowed even into the transit realms of his own Soul. He is, at present, in the Universe of the Wise One – living over and over his many, so very many misdeeds. And with him are his minions who were as sadistic as he. Nor are they alone – but accompanied by many war mongers.

You are aware of this one that I refer to. Names are not required to know the evil in this being. To persecute *any* – any race of people – is so cruel. But who now pays dearly? And not for just a few years – but for eons of time! For he must live through each deed which he perpetrated – each and every one. How many do YOU think he will suffer?

Many with him were even crueler and more sadistic than he. So they pay even more so than he. Nor do those who battled with him go scot free. All pay – right down to the last crumb! I, Soul, say so.

I say that Soul demands that each Soulpart pays the price. All must be accounted for and put to rights – once and for all. No time now for him to have repaid in this Universe. So he is taken elsewhere. But pay he will. Throughout the whole of Soul life, we pay for our misdeeds, as Soulparts on an Earth. Understand, that once a Soulpart leaves the transit realms near to the Earth Plane it then travels along a spiral up into the realms of Soul.

I speak now of atrocities. Only a few, for many are known of by the governments, but not disclosed to man. I tell you of a few of the atrocities perpetrated by this evil one and his minions. What caused them to do such things? Basically, greed, then prestige – self-aggrandisement. Power. Power over others. Power so fearsome – for even their own people at heart were so afraid of their leaders. If *they* had had the courage, they could have overcome and stopped the atrocities. For many had heard of them but, like the ostrich, buried their head so that they could not see or hear – and thought that it would right itself soon.

It never did.

In one town, near to Cologne, lived a Jewish man and his family. He was very wealthy, owning vast amounts of jewels. He did not escape the eye of the evil ones. They took him and cruelly tortured him in front of his family. They took up knives and cut into his body – a little at a time. First a finger, then the nose. Then another finger, then his toes. Then they started on his lower organ and so cruelly tortured him until he died.

The family was so terrified but were held, imprisoned whilst all this brutality went on. Then they too were killed in a like fashion. And all this for a mass of jewels. The man had GLADLY handed over the jewels, but the greedy ones insisted that he and his family had more. This is but one of many similar instances.

As the war progressed against the Jewish race, savagery took hold and camps were set up – as well as special places for torture. Many were literally skinned alive to make them give up their wealth and jewels. – For this race care much for jewels. In time thousands of this Jewish race were put to death. Not all as cruelly as others – but they were shown in no uncertain terms, what these perpetrators thought of them and their ways.

To gently show one how he is greedy and intolerant is one way, but to brutally chastise, is so cruel.

The Soul took compassion on many, and their demise from this Earth was swift – almost momentarily so – and back once more into the transit realms they came. But many of even these Jewish people – as they called themselves – suffered. For in the earlier parts of their lives they too had made others suffer, because of their greed. All pay, in one way, or another.

To this day many bear the scars of this era, and inwardly seeth. No room within them for tolerance. No room within them for, shall I term it, understanding. So, as they return to the realms of transit, they in turn have to pay for all intolerant actions taken out on their persecutors after being persecuted.

Let it be known, without any shadow of a doubt, that each one judges self. None judge another – not even Soul. All must judge self and extract from self, full retribution.

You in this land have thought that you had cause to cheer a leader. But this leader is also in the Universe of the Wise One, being also the cause of many atrocities to occur. Let all understand that war is useless, stupid, and against the way of Soul.

Those who kill shall, in turn, be killed.

This is the Code of Soul.

I speak now of one of our Soul – from the lands of the Core. We have tried to enlighten him, but he is too afraid to listen to our words. He has killed. And in time shall also have the same happen to him. All pay. Even those from our lands.

When we come amongst you, we come as you do – as children born into one family or another. Before coming, we look ahead at the family. Looking to see what obstacles must be overcome. Looking to see what the age ahead is to be like, if man takes this way or that way. We plan the strength to overcome, according to how it will be. But if we accept the greed and intolerance of man we become more man than he. And as bad in many ways, as he.

Not only man, has this one killed in battle, but for pleasure he has killed animals and birds. Life has not been good for him of late for he suffers now in mind and body. Those close to him suffer also, yet they try so hard to help him. Only

Soul can help him. Take the way of value that Soul holds out to you dear one, then all can once again be put to rights – all redeemed – and you could go forward and help mankind.

* * * * *

I speak to you now of a life time of a Soul – the Wise One. This Soul was, as my dear one, in the first place – a Soulpart so strong for his Soul that it was agony if he was prevented from following in the natural way. He quickly assisted his Soul to fulfilment.

Such a gentle one. So gentle. Never a thought of self – always looking at life as something very special. He cared for life. Care, a simple word, but one which meant so much to him. Care? He *adored* his Soul and knew that Soul was all. He knew the majesty of even the simplest being.

Life was Soul. And to him Soul was all that mattered. To him all creatures were beauty – for each was formed, then given the gift of life from Soul. The gift of life. He always respected that gift. Life – the gift of Soul – the gift of gifts – personal to each Being, never to be taken from any.

His Caring for all other Beings whether insects, pests, animals, birds and all – all beings – was such that it came to the notice of the Ultimate.

It was recommended that he become a Soul. But he put it to the Great Ones that they needed more than a Soul. Or rather they needed – more than they needed a Soul – one to give attention to those of a more cruel way of being, than the usual mis-deeder. The way was considered by those of the Core, and this Wise One was invited to join them.

They explained to him their decision and waited for his comment. They had decided, that to have Soulparts of his own – evolving and earning Power for him – would not in any way be correct. That was, if he intended to give to others of evil ways more of his attention than his own Soulparts.

They put forward a method of teaching. This was the method.

All from other Universes that had instigated, and taken the

lead in, any wars against other differing nations – they, never again would be welcomed back into their own Universe. None who condoned, in this fashion, the killing and maiming of others, should go back into their natural habitat.

Let it be understood that I do not in any way allude to those you call soldiers in this age, for they are as sheep led to the slaughter. But I *do* allude to those who lead man or any other type of being into battle.

Such are the governments – the ones who perpetrate war in the first place – for without these governments there would be no war. Neither need the war be between nations – it could also be within a nation.

It was also stipulated that those without courage to finish a lifetime upon Earth – those who committed the act of taking their own life, or even causing such a one to take their own life, those whom you call suicides etc. – they also should never again be allowed in any way near their original Soul again.

Then you have those who are unable in a way to conform to the ideals of Soul. Those who never intend to change their ways. Those who refuse to open their minds – those who deliberately refuse to even listen.

Then you have the, shall I call them, the unfortunate ones. Those who are unable to assist Soul in any way – those who are useless because they will not help themselves. Not so many of these – just a few – but still needing attention.

Those of the Core arranged that, should any of these Soulparts evolve in time, then, they would be given the chance to become a Soul themselves.

The type of teaching that was set out for the parts – who would not be asked, or chosen, but *taken* (by their own actions) into the Universe of the Wise One, was strict without let-up at any time.

The Wise One should arrange that joining it were other Parts from other Souls, also with a like caring, as you might say, for others far different from they. They would assist the Wise One in the teaching and guiding to better ways.

Needless to say, so many offered, and so many had to be turned down. Such is the caring of Souls and Soulparts in the fulfilled realms of Soul.

The teachings, as I say, are strict and constant. The Souls of Might spoke to this Wise One and he went away and decided. His decision coincided with the requirements, and so he and those of the Core gathered and planned how all was to be.

No Earth Plane on this Universe, for no making of Power was required. Each Soul sending a Soulpart to this Universe from its own, would send sufficient Power to sustain the Soulpart whilst it was taught a better way.

The Realms were planned without comfort of any kind. They were planned in stages so to speak. Planned that from the commencing Realm to the final Realm was so gradual in progression in rest of any kind. Only when they had reached the point next to the Wise One in that Universe, could they rest. – No way out what-so-ever until they reached this point.

You of man – you evil and cruel ones – *you* head for this place. There you will see such fear that your atrocities on Earth are as nought! Yes, you will see fear, and you will live through *all* constantly, each and every fear, a million times over.

Neither think that there will not be sufficient room, for it was designed to cater for millions upon millions. Oh yes, there is room alright. Always room enough for you of evil ways – make no mistake there!

I have said that the Realms lack comfort. But that is too nice a way to describe them. For each are so terrible – each one not much better than the next. Each Realm so very gradual in learning. Each a slow agony of mind! Every single aspect of fear is placed before these evil ones – every single one.

Here they learn what it is to fear – but fear more abject

than you can imagine. And this each must face – constantly. None escape. Fear constantly, over and over again. You go to the next realm, but there you meet even more fear. Such evil. Never ending – constant.

All pay. And how they pay! Those who make others afraid – they in turn, will be afraid, and more afraid and more afraid. Horror they face. Creatures so insidious and revolting that you of man would not dare to look upon them. They face all evil.

They face all horror that they doled out to others – and much, much more. They suffer, they pay – for eons upon eons of time they pay. What they have done to others will be done to them – again and again and again!

The Wise One has arranged with the Mighty Ones of the Core that he will adjust the receiving set or brain of each one entering his Universe – so that they cannot turn away at any time. They must without fail observe each lesson as required by Soul to teach them until they leave his Universe. Then a readjustment back to their original way of receiving will be done. None escape.

Beware you murderers. Beware you torturers, beware you animal slayers. Beware you subjugators of all creatures! Those who slaughter will in turn *be* slaughtered, time after time after time.

Mere words, you say. Mere words they are, but they are Truth. Mere words, and mere words cannot describe the agony in this place. Would you, man, care to go to this place? You have the choice. I tell you in Truth – all pay, *all* pay. Turn now to your Soul. Renounce your evil ways. Care as you have never cared before.

How easy it would be to destroy these Soulparts. Yet, that is not the way of Soul. No. That is not the Code of Soul. So the Wise One *gives* to those who only take. He gives of self to those who only want for self. He cares, and cares greatly for those who have no caring – regardless of self!

The Wise One has such strength as to be able to care for

millions of cruel ones and selfish ones. To care with all this viciousness around – to care with those around re-living and re-living, repaying and repaying, *all* the cruelty that they have inflicted upon others – to care with all this viciousness requires *great* strength indeed. Look around your Earth, man, and see the result of just a *few* evil ones!

All in the Universe of the Wise One are taught the hard way constantly. But they *are* taught. I say to you of man, the Wise One is a strong one – so gentle in approach, so caring in all ways. Never judging any, nor allowing any to judge another. For it is to this place that those who have judged others and caused their task on Earth to be halted, have been sent.

And here I do not refer just to those that they have condemned to Death. But I speak of others. I speak of those who have caused such mental anguish to be perpetrated on their victims the so-called criminal. Caused them to undergo treatment in your asylums on Earth, where such ones have been subjected to what is termed "Shock-treatment" to the Brain, and thus prevented that one from receiving in a good way from Soul!

I speak out to you. For whereas others have gone on ahead of you into Soul – where they have joined to Wise One's Universe – *you* have a chance. Not much of a chance to be sure. But a chance for all that. A chance to turn to Soul and renounce your evil ways whilst you are on Earth. That way, depending on how you live the rest of your life on Earth, your Soul will clear away SOME of the damage that you have caused others.

I wonder, will YOU prefer the Universe of the Wise One to your Own?

* * * * *

Soul now relates a story from One who is so Wise in Soul. A young man came to Earth to do a task for his Soul. Came to Earth to earn a little Power for his Soul – easy to do when one is a new Soulpart, for then there is no contamination from another life to contend with.

This young one came, and from the start his parents indoctrinated him with religion and the ways of man – the ways of greed. For all his family had great wealth – none were satisfied. They continually wanted more. Not caring even how they came by it. Treading on all others to get what they wanted, and in the process ruining many a life by their off-hand and callous ways. He was taught to be as they, and so the young one only knew their ways. Until one day he fell in love with a young lady.

She was neither of his religion nor of his class, for she worked, in a small way, on the land. She was lovely – so different to him in every way. His heart danced when he was with her. She was so special – not something to be bought or sold depending on the whim, but someone to cherish. She was his only happiness, she was his all – the one to whom he would give all – his beloved. He adored her and she in turn cared greatly for him.

They met secretly, for he was afraid of what his family would say. The family would not like it. He was torn apart. Torn between being with his loved one and being with the wealth and prestige of the family. There came a time when the young lady could no longer stand the way of intrigue, and asked that he choose either her way or leave her. For it seemed that he was reluctant to take her to his family. He pondered and fretted, putting his beloved one off time and time again from meeting with his family. Until one day the father of the young lady told him that he had sent his daughter away from home.

So this young man in a great rage took up a blade and killed the father of his beloved. When he realised what he had done in anger, he gave himself up to the authorities. But they, knowing who he belonged to, would not listen to his words. They were too afraid of the consequences if they did so. So the young man then took himself to a high cliff – and there threw his life on Earth away.

One lifetime only on the Earth of his Soul, and now he is

in the Universe of the Wise One. No one was there to tell this young man that all is repayed in Soul – in a way of Soul. So in desparation he chose, but chose in ignorance.

Now he pays. It would have been so much easier had he known – and if he had turned to his Soul. Instead, he drove himself from his own Universe – from his own Soul. And he was such a young Soulpart.

None – and let it be known – none who commit suicide can ever again return to their own Soul, and all that remains is for them to be taken into the Universe of the Wise One. There to learn how all must be.

You who interfere cause others distress. You who only want *your* way – your own way – without considering another, could drive them to the realms of the Wise One. You who are the cause of others committing suicide so, also end up in the realms of the Wise One.

To depend on something or someone undependable. To trust someone who is untrustworthy. To look for permanence in something that is temporary.

To do these things always brings disappointment and unhappiness. So it is with man upon Earth at present.

Many say love is the answer. Love is the be-all and end-all – the right thing to do. But like so many of the words which are thrown about in conversation and argument, each person has his own idea as to what it actually means. One person's idea of love may be so very different from that of another.

Some think of love as a duty – a ritual that family, religion or society require – even a fashion. Many see it as a way to gain more wealth and prestige for self. Others look upon love as a way to satisfy the craving for excitment, sex, entertainment, sympathy or security.

Love is not regardless of self. Not a deep feeling of Soul caring. Not clear. You say that love is blind but I ask you, how can you help others to see when you yourself are blind? Be clear of sight. Take off the bandages of non-understanding

– and care *with* understanding. Care, and know that you are as I in Soul – care to help others to see the light of Soul.

They say that love conquers all. But it does not conquer jealousy, nor resentment, nor worry, nor the desire to possess. It does not bring peace of mind.

You sing of love and romance, make poems and stories, you even worship it. But that does not stop the wars and the violence, it does not bring peace on Earth.

Many say that love is the answer to peace – yet their lives have been such a struggle. Many of man have spent their whole lives trying to untangle the so-called mysteries of love – and died with no more of an idea than when they started.

Love is emotion. And emotion prevents man from caring for his fellows in a way of value. It distorts. It judges. It prevents a person from being firm but gentle – which at times is necessary. Love says yes, when it would be caring to say no. Like a child who wants more or a friend who wants sympathy. Love may be to please when it would be more caring to point out a better way.

Many of man think of love as so good, but love at times can be agony – heart-breaking you could say. So often through love, a person does not discover the true intents of another – that is, until it is too late. Then the one on whom you rely, fails you. And once again you feel so lonely – so let down. Love causes such despair – such misery. Even to the extent of killing another being – even to the extent of suicide. Love can be so lonely.

In so many of man's words of love you can see this loneliness – a desperate searching for a companion. Someone to care for him, someone to understand him. One to whom he can give his life, one of beauty and grace of feeling. Who better then to depend upon than your Soul.

None have any need to be lonely. Happiness, contentment, a joy of living, freedom – all these things and more, come from a life spent fulfilling the task for Soul. But only in the fulfilling. So to assist another to do just that *is* to truly care. It is indeed.

You who have loved and lost, now understand the caring that your Soul holds out for you. You who have loved mankind, now can learn to care for mankind. Turn the love that was confused and so often hurtful, to caring. The caring of Soul.

You are as I in Soul. I speak to you now of a Soul. It started as a part of a mighty Soul – one close to the Core of all things, with great understanding of Soul ways. But not in the first place evolving, the young one was sent to be a Soulpart of another mother Soul – that Soul was the Wise One.

Here, under the care and guidance of this wise Soul, the young one evolved. Slowly but surely over the ages of time, the Soulpart learned many ways of being. It saw how to be and how not to be. It saw how futile it is to be afraid, how wrong it is to hurt another in any way.

The young one relinquished all that it ever was after it had earned the right to do so. From the earning, the slate was wiped clean, and it was as though nothing previous had existed – only the Universe of the Wise One. The Soulpart went forward, ever forward. Never looking back at what it was – rather, looking forward to what could be. The young one became older and wiser, evolving and gaining understanding of its new Soul, until eventually the Soulpart became a Soul.

Such is the caring of Soul that it gives so many opportunities to make a fresh start – to forget what has gone on previously and go forward. Even those in the Universe of the Wise One are given the chance.

Yes, they must learn their lesson well – but having done this they can start afresh along the path of understanding, and even become Souls in their own right when sufficient understanding has been earned.

So it was with your own Soul – the one who has nurtured you and put its ways before you. Your own Soul was the Soulpart of my story.

As a Soulpart of the Wise One it knew the qualities of all ways and learned to prefer the qualities of value, so it puts to you now the ways of value as it has always done, in order that you yourselves have free choice in your decision to evolve.

Your Soul now gives you once again the choice to put yourselves to rights within itself – your Own Universe – rather than in the Universe of the Wise One.

Throughout its life as the Soulpart of the Wise One, your Soul saw a wondrous being. – A Soul so strong in its caring that it could teach the cruellest to be so gentle. The Soulpart adored his new Soul, it saw in the Wise One an example, an example that it vowed to live up to no matter what. An example of giving and caring that is beyond words. It was through this caring and this giving that you now exist.

The example was there, and it was taken up by your own Soul. Now the example is placed before all upon this Earth.– Your Own Soul. Your Own Soul – so dearly cared for by this Wise One – has given itself so often for the cause of others. And yet when it comes to fulfilling itself instead, it still gives to its Soulparts so that they have a chance of evolving – even before their own Soul is fulfilled. Such a giver is this Soul of yours.

You have a Soul to admire. You have indeed. A Soul so caring that it would rather be folded in than stop giving to its Soulparts. I know of no better example of caring – not in all the Universes. Cherish that example dearly – your Own Soul. You are as I in Soul.

* * * * *

You, dear scribe, can now prepare yourself to relate from my dear friend in Soul – The Wise One. I refer to him by this name for to us he *is* a Wise One. I speak to you as though he himself relates to you. But you, dear scribe, know that only I can send your thoughts.

I tell you – I tell you of mankind this, for it is so. In all Truth it is so.

None other than your own dear Soul, can speak mentally with you. Let none try to tell you otherwise. Should they endeavour to do so, I say that they shall pay dearly in the days ahead, for to frighten another is wrong, and Soul now extracts payment. Let that be clearly known.

We who come to your Earth speak how all is and how all has been – not only on your Earth but throughout the lands of Soul. We speak Truth. We speak of goodness and of evil – no white-washing here.

I tell you a story of great caring yet a story of great cruelty. I show you that even in Soul, only caring is the way to go forward. It was a unique occurrence never to be repeated – never allowed to be repeated. This is the story of a Soul – not a Soulpart, but a Soul. For once, in many ages of time past, a newly created Soul set out on its way to fulfilment. It was unique in a way – infamous you could call it, for *this* Soul forgot to care.

All started in a good way. The plan for the Universe was a good one. All thought that this Soul would have no trouble in its fulfilment. We, the Souls of the Core, saw no reason to encroach in any way – for the Power came along the line at the right time and in the allotted way. This one was strong for Soul, and was determined to assist by making its share of the Power.

But there was one weakness which it kept secret within itself, and this weakness caused the whole Universe to fail. Understand, that when Souls first set out their Universes, they are all weak in one way or another, until practice, in a way, makes perfect – so to speak. They lack experience *as* a Soul, but learn as their Universe progresses. They learn how to control – (shall I put it) – their Universe in a better way.

Therefore many times it may be necessary to discuss

problems with both the Ultimate, and mighty, more experienced Souls. This can be done at a moment's notice, and each and every one are always willing to give assistance if required – as in your Universe.

This Soul wanted to go it alone. It wanted to play its part in the linkage and put this at the top of its list, instead of caring. Remember, all is one, and each work for the good of the whole. None can separate themselves. Souls are taught to care for all others, be it Soulparts or Souls, for by this caring the Power is assured.

It was as though a reversal took place within this Soul, for at first caring was its intention – but once the reversal took place it was the task of that particular Soul to inform the Ultimate of the fact. Yet the Soul tried alone to put to rights what it did not have the inner Power to do so. And after failing in its attempt, it went from bad to worse. Rather like man in a way – not wanting to show his most precious friend that he is in need.

All on the surface seemed well. – The Power was sent regularly along the linkage to the Ultimate. All was calm – no turmoil – no writhing of the Spiral.

We waited and waited, and waited. Waited in the region of a million years by your standards, but no time at all by ours. But there was something wrong. Something which caused the Souls of the Core to send a probe of Power (undetected by the Soul) into the Universe. For this Universe was not growing, not expanding – this Soul was not fulfilling itself in any way.

What we found there was desolation. No beauty whatsoever – all was barren and harsh – such an eye-sore. On this hell of a place were Soulparts, so crowded, for there was no caring or comfort, nor relief from boredom – the Soul gave no freedom of choice, and the Soulparts just followed without any will of their own, just like puppets – exactly as the Soul directed. No chance of rest or of refusing a task. Instant annihilation was the reward to any refusing the Soul. This *was* a Powerhouse. The Power was made all right, but at the expense of many Soulparts. There was no joy whatsoever in this Universe – none evolving into higher realms to share with the Soul all that there is.

Such brutality to those of ours.

Thus it was, that this Soul – because it was not caring of its Soulparts in *any* way – was slowly but surely, killing itself. For that is what it did when it destroyed parts of itself. Such crass stupidity, such cruelty. This Soul – which had once been so caring – had become so vicious.

It was like the oriental child who VOLUNTARILY chooses to bind her small feet when young, but then leaves the wrappings on as she grows up. Thus, great pain does she inflict upon herself, yet she does not dare to take off the bandages and see the ugliness within. She does not want others to see the damage that she has done to herself, but knows that only by removing the bandages can the pain stop and the foot grow in the correct way.

It was like the heavy smoker or the alcoholic. All know the damage that they cause to themselves but do not want to admit their failings to the ones who *can* help – do not even admit that they *want* help. Nothing goes away of its own accord.

So all was in a dilemma – but such a cruel and vicious dilemma. For this Soul not only destroyed and stunted *itself*, but it also did the same to living beings – beings with feelings – beings that it created in the first place! How can a mother feel if, after having given birth to, and raised children – she then kills them off or tortures them? How stupid and callous. How anti-Soul. Soul does not break down, it builds up. Soul gives and in the giving gains much comfort and well-being. How far better it is for the mother to care for them and teach the children in turn, to care.

But, you may say, why am *I* telling you this? What has it to do with my Universe of "mis-fits" and "repayers"? Have I not said, that all must pay the price – even Souls.

It was decided that this Soul should be set as an example to all other Souls. So the Souls of might gathered together and folded in the Universe. The Soul was taken down in size and Power to no larger, no better – than a Soulpart. He was then taken and placed amongst the evil ones in my Universe, there to live over and over all – and I repeat all – of the cruelty which he gave out to others.

In all our time as Souls – over the billions of years – nought like this had occurred before. Only this one Soul has ever had to be reprimanded. Never again will such a thing happen. For now, in each Universe, we have a constant probe – a probe which does not affect the running of the Universe in any way, but whose presence even a mighty Soul is not aware of.

And what of the Soulparts?

The Soulparts are safe – safe and happy, even though they have lost their Soul. But now they have a new Soul. For these Soulparts were set in a new Universe with a wondrous Soul to care for them. All is good here, they have all they desire – no longer asked even to earn for Soul. They have learned to be caring, for they are set a good example – indeed they are. All is peace and harmony, and their new Soul adores them so much. Yes, this wondrous Soul took them to it – and taught, cherished and nurtured these Soulparts of another's Soul. This is indeed a great one.

Soul cares – cares for all beings – all life. To those who have been deprived we give, for none shall suffer at the expense of Soul.

Do you care – care for all beings – all life? Like this wondrous Soul, would you care for ones different from yourself in many ways? Would you, man, even care for ones *as* yourself? Mankind is in need of your help! Do you care enough to assist – care enough to assist your own Soul – care enough to even assist yourself?

These Soulparts – through the gentleness and caring of this mighty Soul – have, in turn, learned to care. For they have now asked that their own Soul be allowed another chance to be with them again, so that they, in turn, can care for it in a good way. They have asked for the one who treated them so cruelly – the one who deprived them of all goodness. Yes, *they* have learned to care and respect life of all kinds. Could you do this? Could you forgive? Could you care for those who treated *you* so badly? – Yet not nearly so badly as this cruel Soul to its Soulparts.

In time – in ages to come – providing this Soul redeems itself, then all shall once again be linked together. For all must learn that all pay the price – even Souls.

Soul builds up, it never destroys.

But will you man, destroy yourselves?

How can any help those who do not wish to be helped?

You of man have been given a chance – a last chance to be sure – but still a chance.

I, Soul, say so.

CHAPTER FOUR

I now take you back through the beginning of time – through the start of this Universe – through the start of all the Universes in the lands of Soul. I take you back to the point in this area of space (or dimension, you could say) when all began.

I moved, sensing the Mass that was myself. Sensing the place that I was in – the land which was so new to me. I existed – moving, pulsing, living, throbbing like the beats of a million hearts. There I remained. Still – unmoving after the explosive entry into the area of space which I now found myself. The newness was strange at first. It was strange to suddenly become aware. But it was a limited kind of awareness, one of watching and waiting, scanning within and without.

There was none other save the Mass that was myself. I was alone – dreadfully alone. Such a silence, such an unknowing, such a loneliness. There was no other who could help – no other who could tell me what I was – no other to give me a way. Just a nothingness.

Eons of time passed without knowing. The loneliness was unbearable. So unbearable that a point was reached when in despair I let out a sound. A cry which echoed back and forth within the surrounding space. A cry of desolation. On and on it went, back and forth, back and forth until the cry faded. And once again there was silence. A stunned silence.

It was again many eons until I became clear of sense. Then once again I looked within. What I saw was different – there had been a change. Not so much a "physical" change as a change of awareness. There was a feeling of achievement – the knowledge that I had done something. I looked closer within myself to see what I was, and found – substance. A substance vastly different to that around. A substance that acted upon itself so as to be increasing. I was Power.

But there was more than just Power. There was something within which I had not previously been aware of. Something which gave rise to order within disorder. Something which controlled Power. That something was Intelligence.

This discovery (this awakening in a way) was the real start of understanding myself. Of understanding who I was, where I had come from, how I was. I began to realise what Power coupled with Intelligence, could achieve.

The Power of myself, I found, was awesome – so vast and unyielding – so clumsy and brutal. But now with Intelligence, the Power could be gentled, guided, manipulated – even changed from one form to another.

During this stage of understanding my own capabilities so to speak, I decided that it was not enough to know what I was. It was necessary to have a purpose. So I looked out from myself, looking beyond the land which I occupied to the lands adjoining. There I saw other beings – beings so different to the Mass that was I. Some were of great beauty, others of a more ugly nature, but nevertheless they were beings – beings in their own right – beings which deserved respect. The lands too varied greatly. Some were so desolate, others were places of great harmony and purpose.

Having seen the beings of other lands, I also determined to take part of myself and create beings. By carefully taking a part of the Mass and separating it from the whole, I found that this caused the substances in the area in which it was placed to be changed. And after a series of experiments as you might say, it became clear that although many substances could be formed from the surrounding substance, the separating of parts of myself from the Mass caused these parts to disintegrate.

Seeing that this placing apart process was in no way satisfactory, I then separated parts of myself into beings *within* the Core – or the body of Mass. This method proved successful and after a few attempts a type of being was developed which would exist by a way of giving, regardless of self.

So it was that the first Soul was created – created of the Core of Power which is the Mass. Yet within the Mass.

The Soul would give to the Core what Power it had in excess of its requirements, and the Core in turn would process and multiply that Power, then return it – in the form of an Essence – to the Soul. This Essence would then be used by the Soul to create new beings of itself. These beings or Soulparts could then evolve to such a stage that they in turn were made a Soul.

All Souls are linked to be as one. All giving what is theirs to give. Each acting for the good of the next – regardless of self.

I came into a way of being without understanding what I was. You could say I came from nowhere. And at first it seemed so, until many ages of time later when I had found a way or two out of what was nought, into a way of value.

You can only comprehend as much as the Power and Intelligence of your own Soul allows you to. I am all that exists in this land that I call Soul, but within what I am I have many ways of being. I teach Truth of all I am, to you, if you care to listen to the words of my scribe. He in Soul is as I. No other way for him to be, for he is I in every way. Whilst on Earth he inhabits, by thought, a cocoon of the substance of this *your* Universe – but his thoughts are mine. Never forget that when he speaks with you. For as he speaks to you so you hear my words – none other than I.

I place before you many stories – all of Truth – from this age, or that civilisation, and I say to you, you are able to evolve into a better way than ever before – but only if you take notice of the way all truly is. Many are on this Earth here to assist man in Value *not* rubbish. Care for them, for they are your only salvation. Only through the words of

Soul can man benefit now. No other way is possible now. Every time that you think otherwise, watch the results, and you will know who speaks Truth. You are as I.

I have told you of the very beginning – shown you how the Mass that is I grew from a mere speck, to a being of great Power and Intelligence – how I evolved to be what I am.

It is important that you realise why evolving in a way of value is so necessary for you of man upon Earth. I care that you evolve. I care that you understand yourselves and understand the way you are in reality. So I now put to you a way of evolving – a story of one who was as you naturally are in so many ways.

This is the story of a life and a death. The life and death of a Soulpart.

The birth was on an Earth – not this Earth of man's, but in another Universe ages of time past. He was part of a mighty Soul.

Right from the very start this one was strong for Soul, and he unlike man at present, only needed one stay of earning for his Soul on the Earth of its Universe. All throughout that life he eagerly followed the way of his Soul and by doing this was so happy and contented.

Gentleness was the key. Gentleness was the way that he was strong. Only Soul mattered to him – never self. This Soulpart LIVED for Soul – none other save his Soul. He knew that by caring for his Soul, he was caring for all on that Earth and all in that Universe.

This life was how a life on Earth should be lived – no striving, no discomfort of mind or body. Calmness pervaded within and without. He saw how if you trust your Soul, then you want for nought. Each day was a delight to live, a chance to give so much caring to those around – a chance to learn so much – a chance to give what was learned, to others. It was so interesting. There were so many new ideas and new avenues to explore. He was just amazed at all the wonders that unfolded every moment of his life.

But Always – he looked to his Soul for example. And what a good example it was. So caring of each and every one of its Soulparts, giving always what was best for them. Many different means did the Soul use to show its Soulparts that only by respect, tolerance, and gentleness can any thing of value be achieved. His Soul taught by example, and always allowed its parts to choose whether or not to follow the example. It gave and gave and gave without any thought of the cost. But all had to be earned. All had to want value before they would be given value.

Having completed his task on the Earth, the Soulpart returned to the wondrous realms of Soul. These are such joyous places to be in, for here it is impossible to be intolerant or disrespectful in any way, all emotion melts into nothingness. There is such peace and contentment.

After ages of time, he evolved throughout all the realms of his Soul – constantly striving to do his best in every way to understand all that there was to understand. He learned well for it was so interesting. Even the way each aspect of understanding unfolded was such a joy to him – let alone the understanding itself!

He lived many lives on many differing Earths, and experienced both the good and the bad, both selfishness and selflessness. He saw all the ways to be, as well as the ways *not* to be. The learning and evolving as so gradual and uplifting, for in Soul, none are thrown head first into the deep end so to speak. Each Soulpart who wishes to evolve is only set tasks – be it on an Earth or in Soul – that it is capable of completing.

What this Soulpart would not do for his wondrous Soul! With respect, he gratefully accepted all that Soul put his way. For he knew that all was done for a very good reason, and always for his own benefit. His strength was great – but only because he would give of it to others, regardless of self. Such strength and courage of caring he had.

In one lifetime that he spent on the Earth of his own Universe, it was his task to bring the Soulparts there to a better way of being. So returning once again to the place that had been a start for *him* in ages past, he showed them that Soul does not waste in any way. For to waste is to be uncaring of the effort that Soul has put into the necessities for life on Earth.

In this task he was so successful that, after a few generations, no more Power was needed, and there was no requirement for the Earth any longer. So all the Soulparts came home and the Earth was folded in. For once the Soul is fulfilled then all in the Universe from that time forward, can rest and enjoy whatever Soul places for them. Unless they, like this particular Soulpart, are eager to earn even more glory for Soul.

Never once did he in Soul realms consider self, but put Soul first, last, and at all times.

Thus it was decided amongst the highest Powers in Soul to honour this Soulpart by making him a Soul in his own right. But he asked first to be allowed to assist in the way of turning mankind towards his Soul.

Over the millions of years, he came back and forth to the Earth of man – many times man listened to his words, many times he did not. But always man would turn back to his selfish and uncaring ways. So now he is on Earth again, in one final attempt to turn man to his Soul – he, along with many other mighty Souls and Soulparts come to give you for the last time, the words of Soul.

It was on your Earth in this lifetime that this Soulpart died.

Eons of time had passed and he never once reminded the great ones in Soul of their promise to make him a Soul. So, in his absence on the Earth of man in this lifetime, they have linked him – this one who was always strong for Soul – to the most honoured Soul of all. For this Great Soul had closed down its own Universe so that Soulparts would not be invaded by other beings – beings of great evil who have no thought for those of our lands.

A new lineage was set up in Soul, linked to this most honoured of Souls.

And the Soulpart of my story became a Soul.

Together, these two have the means of fulfilling the requirements of Soul – constantly.

So the one who was taught became the teacher. And the Soulpart who looked to an example then became an example himself. Where there was one to care for, then there were millions. And where he was given, now he most give. As a Soulpart he cared for his Soul above all else – now he cares for his own Soulparts with no thought of self. They must learn as he has, to care to give and to be gentle.

Respect he demands, and respect he is given. For each and every Soulpart must learn that, with respect, Soul *is* All. He is always ready to assist, ever watching, ever guiding, ever giving of himself. Through him his Soulparts are uplifted and sustained. They adore their mighty Soul and he adores them, he does indeed.

So it is with the Soul of mankind. Turn to it for there is so much to learn and earn. Be a user of thought instead of a waster of thought. Be a Soul in your own right. Your Soul waits to give such value, such Truth.

This story is a true one. Ask my scribe. Ask the one who became the thought of a Soul instead of the thought sent to a Soulpart.

The Soulpart of my story is now more as I than the Soul it was born of – not yet in valour, but in strength of Soul. It is now nearer to the Core of Power in its new lineage. It has taken its place with the Souls who decide all things – and this is only reserved for those worthy of the position. Only strength do we tolerate.

But the strength is so gentle that to an onlooker elsewhere, it is as though we are so weak. It is necessary for us to appear so. For to show others – and there *are* others in differing places than ours – to show them that we are strong would mean that they too would start to become stronger.

As on this Earth of man it occurs that gentle ones for a time are left alone. They cannot harm a strong one – or so it is thought! So we play possum in a way, until we are ready and COMPLETELY fulfilled. Mankind is preventing us from naturally becoming fulfilled. He is the cancer within the body of Soul.

We would rather it be in a natural way. That way we know all has been earned and not given. It complies with the Code that we have sent ourselves to follow – the Code of Soul.

I set it out for you now.

To give, regardless of self.
To serve, regardless of self.
To, with all our Power, strive to bring gentleness and caring to all – regardless of self.
To put all our Power at the disposal of all so that all in our Souls can benefit – constantly, regardless of self.
To uphold the Core of Power, regardless of self.
To care, regardless of self.

You, dear scribe, in Soul have promised the Ultimate that this is your way. I say, so be it.

You are as I.

When Souls use this greeting it means that each and every one complies with the Code of Soul. No Soul is without complying or making in the first stages, an attempt to try to fulfil. Mankind, *your* Soul promised to adhere to the Code of Soul. But to do so requires its Soulparts also to follow suit – to follow the Code of Soul. I Soul, adhere to the Code of Soul. My thought – my scribe – is as I, and so also abides by my way. So it is with all those who come to you from the Souls of the Core – each and every one caring, regardless of self. All that we say and do will be by, and within, this Code. Soul cares for you of mankind. Cares enough to give you one last chance to redeem yourselves. Soul once again comes to your Earth to show gentleness, respect and caring. But now it comes in force. Such great strength that you of mankind have never seen before, nor will ever again. But the strength can be gentle. The strength can be caring. But strength it will be, nevertheless!

All depends upon you of mankind – we will play our part, but will you?

Take strength from us. Take strength from our words and deeds. Then go forward with Soul, to glory unbounded.

In Soul each cares for the next. All give freely and thus benefit by each others experiences. Only because Soul is one can this exchange occur. Soul is therefore both sameness and difference. Sameness in objective and way of being – different in age and experience. This is also the case with man on Earth when he turns to his Soul.

In Soul, each is a companion to the next because each gives to the next, freely, caringly. It is by this giving – this caring regardless of self – this companionship – that Souls evolve. No other way. It is by this way that you on Earth can evolve.

Soul provides companions upon Earth so that you can give value to them. Indeed in many instances you have others about you – in work, in the home, or just friends whose company you enjoy in life, even animals. All these are your companions – all are put your way so that you can enjoy each other.

But when I say companions I do not mean someone to own or possess, rather someone to care for and to allow free choice as to what they wish to do, and where they wish to go. Nor do I mean one who would possess you and prevent you from following *your chosen way*. To be secretive or deceptive is in no way being a companion. Only when there is truth – absolute truth, constantly – can there be companionship. Only then are there no obligations, or commitments – only then is there freedom.

To be a companion – even to allow others to truly care

for you – you must give. Give caring, truth, understanding and free choice. That is most important. Not just to a selective few – to favourites – but to all. After all, it is easy to care for those who care for you, but it is another matter to care and give to those who don't. To enjoy true companionship is so good, whether it be between man and man, man and woman, or between you and your Soul. So good to share a smile or a laugh. So good to give a kind word or a gentle touch. Remember, only by being a companion with your own Soul can you be a companion to *any* of man.

Man needs companionship. Any being needs companionship. – Someone to talk to and exchange experiences and understanding. But it is necessary to care. It is necessary to give of value. Care by being gentle, tolerant and respectful, for only then can any exchange occur. Give of value by using the thoughts of Soul to capacity.

Soul gives – constantly. You are Soul. Therefore it is by your very nature that only if you give can you possibly gain any satisfaction or understanding. Similarly to enjoy companionship it is necessary to give of value for only if you do this can you expect to receive anything of value in return. Give of value by giving of your Soul – all caring, all tolerance.

At present, man relies upon others of man for companionship. This is the case with the wife, the husband, the family or a group of friends or acquaintances. It is only because he ignores his lifelong and ever present companion – his Soul – that this is necessary. A companion by definition, is as you in many ways. What better companion could there be therefore, than your real self – your Soul?

Place now the emphasis off man-to-man companionship and on to man-to-Soul companionship. By doing this you open up a whole new avenue of knowledge, understanding, ideas and experiences. By doing this you first of all benefit. Then secondly, those of man around you benefit – and I mean *truly* benefit. No longer be lonely. No longer be frustrated because none give of value. Soul gives – constantly. Be your own companion by turning to your Soul. Allow your Soul to be your companion.

Life *would* be monotonous if there were no exchanges of new ideas and information. But this need not only occur among man. It should also occur between you and your intelligence – you and your creator and benefactor – you and your Soul.

Any being needs a companion in order to learn from and to give to. But companionship is a two way process. For how can any be your companion if you choose to ignore them, and how can you be their companion if they choose to ignore you? It is necessary for *both* parties to give and to care before any companionship can develop. None can ever have a companion when they are selfish, for then they never *want* a companion – merely a body or a slave. It is because man is selfish that he never enjoys the benefits of true companionship.

Soul wishes to be your companion constantly, but is brushed aside when you choose selfish ways. Allow your Soul to care for you and give you value so that you in turn may care and give of that value to others. If you do this, you then start on the way to peace on Earth and goodwill to all men.

Many will reject such ways of companionship, for many like to own and to possess. But there are those who will be strong for truth and freedom. These few strong ones will be few at first – and to these few I will give all. In some eyes they will be looked upon as cruel – but only by those who want their own way and cannot get it. In some eyes they will be looked upon as cold and uncaring – but only by those who want to be pleased and pampered. But in my eyes, they will be so dear.

In my eyes they will be the few courageous ones to lead. To them, I WILL GIVE ALL.

Companionship. It takes courage to be a companion instead of a captive or a captor.

Care for Soul by allowing it to be your companion. Give

to Soul by caring for all. And care for all by being respectful, tolerant and gentle – as you are in Soul.

You are as I in Soul.

Be so on Earth.

CHAPTER FIVE

The beings that invaded us are about to have the same occurrence done to them. But if any anywhere have any semblance of care we without doubt shall take them into what we are, and nurture them as we would do one of our own beings. I know that this cannot be for I have used every means of identifying with them – but all to no avail.

Invading the invader is child's play to me – it only requires that all of myself is braced against them. But one opening would allow them infiltration, and once that occurs it means that I must then close down completely that which is affected.

Now liken the beings to a cancer within the body of man, that can remain undetected until so much damage is done that the way of the cocoon is rotted with the workings of the cancer.

In the early stages it can be cut away, but in the later stages it has so taken a hold, as to strangle and to suffocate the mechanism of the cocoon.

It requires understanding that the shape and ways of man are so totally differing from the beings. It requires to be also known that so much is the multiplication that some of the divided ones – even near to our lands – are so tiny in size as to be no larger than the head of a match.

They cannot multiply much more and be noticed by us – so we must out with them or our existence is also in danger from their contaminations. Indeed, they already have overrun and destroyed out of Eternity, other beings from other lands.

You understand now the position – but if you consider that I attack with no just cause you are mistaken in your ideas. None shall suffer – that is what will occur – all put through the way of the filter, quickly and expertly into dust-like particles.

The way that the beings are is in no way like the way of Souls – to us they are as other types of dense substance, dross. I have given every consideration to the way they are and now I must act, otherwise each and every one of you must perish along with me – the Mass. I, who was made by one of them, that had at one time Intelligence so great, that it made what is I.

Do you think that I wipe out these beings for no good reason? I would nurture them to myself if I could find one aspect of caring there in any way – not destroy what they are. I say that it is time to see all as it really is – not as man's concept of cruelty is. Soon there would be no rhyme nor reason in any land (whether ours or others) if they overreach what I am.

Such is the position. And now I speak to you of a matter that greatly concerns you of man. That is, the way of Power.

Souls are arranged that they convert the dross of substance into Power. Indeed a Soul's shape and layout are designed specifically to do this. Souls chew away at dross, and convert it into a lighter way of substance which can be used by the Mass that is I. A Soul *is* a Universe – and each Soul is set a task of attacking a certain area and type of dross.

A Universe is set out in the shape of a cone or a spinning top. It has a point which attacks the dross, and an apex or seat of Soul. In the early days of its existence, a Universe is very thin and pointed, but as dross is converted to Power the apex swells out making the whole Universe cone-like. At the very base of the Universe, the point – or stylus – tracks in a circular pattern over that area of dross that it has been given to chew away. The way of the Stylus determines the pattern upon the dross. Compare this action with the moving of a drill over a concrete surface. The spinning action of the *whole* Universe enables the Stylus to stay in contact with the dross – rather like the forward movement of a screw when turned into a wall.

The movement of the chewed substance from base to apex

is in the way of a spiral. This movement causes the Universe to grow in Power, and as the weight of Power increases so does the spiral. It is this increase or swelling of the spiral that ensures a perpetual spin of the Universe.

At the very base of the Universe, the Stylus acts upon the dross as would an electric razor. – The point or Stylus comprising of a filter, an Earth, its atmosphere and its outer rim. The outer part – the filter – can be likened to a mesh on the razor. This filter does not turn with the Universe but remains stationary against the dross.

Rubbing against the dross which comes through the filter is the outer rim of an Earth. By its close movement over the filter and its own spinning action, the outer rim breaks down the dross even further.

Understand that when I say outer rim I do not mean the actual surface of the Earth. Rather it is the layer which man with *his* Earth calls "the burn-up". This layer surrounding the atmosphere of the Earth is – in its normal function – so bright and warming as it rubs against the dross. So much so that it provides all the light and heat necessary for the Soulparts to live upon the Earth. You could liken this outer rim to the cutting and Grinding edges of the razor.

I now come to the way of an Earth.

It is on an Earth that the Soul of a Universe places its Soulparts. These Soulparts live by eating the soil of the Earth in the form of vegetation. As I have stated previously it is their task to use the machine of the cocoon to process dross. You may be asking yourselves how it is, that the finely ground up dross from the outer rim, comes through the Earth's atmosphere and into the vegetation that is to be eaten. But I put it to you. What on *your* Earth does vegetation require other than a moist rich soil ? What else is required for growth?

Heat.   Light.

All plants require heat and light. So it is that the dross from the outer rim comes to the Earth in the way of heat and light. Such a natural way – so soothing to the Soulparts on Earth.

The friction, you could say, of the outer rim against the dross, causes such fine particles of dross to fall down like rain upon the Earth. Even in their travels through the Earth's atmosphere, the particles are made finer. As this occurs, the atmosphere is warmed and made lighter.

Heat and light *are* particles, but so very fine. You on this Earth can feel the heat upon your skin on a sunny day, and you can see if you look closely, the dross particles moving in the atmosphere about you. Viewed from a great distance above the Earth's surface, the atmosphere itself has at times a glow of its own.

I continue on the way of explaining the conversion of dross to Power.

A moist rich soil – that is the key. After all, if the soil is poor and sandy, very little grows upon it – even with heat and light. So how is it that a rich soil can come about, you may ask?

In the natural way of things, the Soulparts on an Earth take from the soil the food that grows there. Then their task proper begins. They, by the use of the machine which is the body or cocoon, process the dross into an even finer, and more pliable substance. By this I mean that they eat the dross which is the vegetation. The cocoon works upon the vegetation and then Outputs the final chewed product. The Soulparts, by their placing of this Output into the soil of the Earth, enables the Power-making process to continue.

With man on this Earth at present he fails to use his cocoon in the way intended, and so ruins his body and his Earth, in the following ways.

The cocoon of man was meant to take into it the natural vegetation of the Earth. It was not intended to take in a mass of chemicals, a great mixture of foodstuffs, and the flesh of other living beings. Nor was it intended to be thrown about and worried as it is.

The body is a delicate machine and should be looked after in the correct way. Your Soul has provided a multitude of foodstuffs for you to eat – fruits, cereals, fish and vegetables. But have care in eating even these, because the juices of the stomach and digestive tracks are specific in their action – and by mixing differing foods you cause these juices to be ineffective.

Likewise if you dilute the juices with other liquids. Far better to eat your fill of one particular food – say cabbage (if you care, with a little wholesome bread) – and then take a drink of water at a later time. By eating in such a simple way you will alleviate the problems of over weight and indigestion. By eating the flesh of animals, birds or insects, you bring upon yourself much trouble, for parasites within their flesh can – and *do* – cause cancerous growths to form in the cocoon of man. Such a stupid way to eat the beings which are sent to your Earth to assist in the way of Powering your Universe.

Not only does man at present mistreat his body, he also fails to make use of its output. Instead of placing his urine and excretia into the soil, he washes it away with water – making the output useless, and making his Earth and seas smelly and disease ridden. Such a waste when his Earth is crying out for the nourishment that is so badly needs.

I have mentioned previously moist rich soil. Now look around at your Earth at present, and what do you see ? One thing that you see very little of is moist rich soil. No. Most is poor rocky, sandy soil and deserts, and *also* seas. What little land remains above water is so dry and crumbly – so un-fertile even with the useless chemicals that man puts into it.

But there is a way to make all fertile – to have once again moist fertile soil. It is by a natural way, a simple way. I now speak out of this way for all to hear – all, not just a few "experts" or those who can pay high prices. I speak out to all of man, for it concerns each and every one. Every one in every country – from the darkest to the palest of skin, from the most rich to the most poor. It concerns all of man – all, regardless of class or creed.

* * * * *

Man eats, then he outputs from the body, urine and excretia. These body products should be placed directly into the soil and covered over immediately with more soil.

* * * * *

That is it. No more, no less. That is the way man earns Power for his Soul. That is the way he fertilises his soil. By adding any chemicals or water to the output – by not covering over with more soil – by allowing the output to ferment before using – by doing all these things the output is ruined.

But by placing the output into the soil in the correct manner, man breaks up the hardness and gives nourishment to the soil. If the ground is then left awhile (a matter of a month or so, with output from one who ate in the correct way – a matter of a year or so from one who ate meat etc.). – if the ground is left for a while so that the output dissolves into the soil, then you will find that it yields good crops and holds within itself much warmth and much moisture.

After all, it has been through man's neglect of the soil and his pressing down upon it, that the moisture has been squeezed out of it to form the oceans that you now see upon your Earth.

This simple and easy process of man placing his output into the soil in the correct manner, this simple thing is of the *greatest importance* to you of man and to your Soul. This way determines whether you go forward in evolving or whether you annihilate yourselves – it is that important.

There are only two possible pathways to go. Either the Soulparts that are man earn for their Soul towards its fulfillment, or else the Soulparts neglect their Soul and it has to close down this Earth and Universe through lack of Power. So now the time is short, and I – along with your Soul –

86

place before each and every one of man, the way of Soul. We give each of man every opportunity to take a better way — of that you can be so sure. But this is the last chance for man.

He can care for his Soul by earning Power for it, or he can annihilate himself from his Soul to the Universe of the Wise One. That is the choice that is before each one of man.

I have mentioned previously that man's task on Earth is two-fold. And I have attempted — within the limitation of words of a book — to give you an idea of the first part:— evolving for self. But in this chapter I bring to your notice the second and more important aspect. That is, the creating of the all important Power for your Soul.

Even without caring to evolve for self in the ways of thought, your Soul — in this instance — has deemed that merely by placing your output into the Soil, in the correct way, your task will be said to be completed — and your future assured. All then will be made easy for you — both on Earth, in a life free from troubles, and in the *true realms* of Soul after your stay on Earth.

I repeat so that you are in no doubt of my meaning. By just placing the bodily output — the excretia and urine — into the soil in the correct way, you fulfil all that is required for your task upon Earth. I will now explain how by doing this, you Power your Soul.

In the natural way of things man places his output into the ground. Over a period of time — dependent on the condition of the output and the condition of the Earth — this output is dissolved into the Earth. Whilst in the Earth it is chewed upon by the actions of the Earth to become finer and finer in texture — descending deeper into the Earth as it does so. The output goes through various stages of substance. It first goes into a peat like substance, then — as it slowly descends — into coal, then oil. It finally ends up in the way of gas and gradually collects in the underground cavities specially made for this purpose. Because the Earth of man has now been compressed by constant mis-use over the last four million years, you are now able to see many such cavities exposed on the surface.

It is necessary, when considering what I say, to reverse many of your present ideas. Take the coal, oil and gas of the Earth for example. Each burn to one degree or another. Each give off heat and light when burned. Taking the Gas – the way of substance that is the finest – the way that is almost Power itself. The Gas is so fine and light in texture and when burned gives much heat and light, yet the finest of waste products. With the oil and coal you end with more coarse waste products such as fine powders or ashes.

But you always get *heat* and *light*.

Realise that by burning the natural products of the Earth you are wasting – in fact reversing – the way of converted dross to Power. Heat and light come only from Output – that is the only way. So easy for man to burn up and destroy what his Soul uses to keep *him* in existence.

Man has never been able to produce light without heat – without friction. No other way is possible on your Earth. That is because heat *is* light. And light is heat.

I know how you can have heat and light without spending one cent of your precious money, but whether you will listen to my words and believe them is another matter.

In the natural way of things, the Gas builds up in the cavities over the years, until such a time as the pressure is so great that the Soul arranges the Gas to come to the surface of the Earth. By way of volcanoes and other such openings from below, the Gases burst forth high into the atmosphere. The pressure and friction of the Gas upon the passageways to the surface is so great that it causes rock to melt and spew out to the surface. No truth in the tale that the Earth below is molten hot.

If man listened to his Soul – as he did in the early days – he would know when and where a volcano was to errupt, and be able to move away to safety. Just as do the birds and other animals which are able to move when Soul directs.

Soul guides man in many ways if he allows it to do so – if he listens to his thoughts.

I continue on the way of Power. But as I do, realise that I first speak of how things were in the early days of this Universe – and how things are in other Universes. For all is much changed now in this Universe of yours – not in a natural way at all. In the early days, the Gas was thrown upwards through the atmosphere to the outer rim. By the way of salt and another substance, the Gas perculated through the outer rim and through the filter which surrounds the Stylus at the base of the Universe. Through this filtering, the Gas is made so pure that it is then Power.

You could liken the filter, the outer rim, the atmosphere, and the Earth itself to spheres or shells spinning within each other. And liken the whole of this – the Stylus – to the ball-bearing in a ballpoint pen. Rather like the idea man has had (but mis-used) of what *he* calls "atoms". Only the lower three quarters of the filter (a bowl shape) is in contact with the dross to be worked upon.

You may see from my explantion, that the spheres work in both directions so to speak, that is, grinding down the dross on its way *to* the Earth, and purifying the Gas to Power on its way *from* the Earth. This is most necessary for at times the beings which try to smother our lands can be so small as to be undetectable at first – and only when they have chance to grow within the dross can we detect and destroy by a burning with Soul Power. I arrange that there are many safeguards against Souls and Soulparts being invaded.

The Power collects on the upper surfaces of the filter – the part of it not in contact with the dross. It is collected by the moon which passes close by, gathering the Power to itself for transfer to transit realms. The glowing Power settles upon the moon in specially shaped containers – craters – for its journey to the planets. For the Planets *are* the transit realms.

The way of the base – and remember, I now speak of the

natural way of things – the way of the base is fast moving. The moon quickly gathers much Power and then speeds off to the nearest transit realm or planet.

On completion of its task upon Earth, the Soulpart accompanies the Power which it has earned for itself. And both it and the Power are transferred into the planet by way of fissures upon the surface. Once a planet has been filled with the Soulparts and their Power, it quickly speeds off up the spiral of Soul. When this occurs another planet comes in its place – ready to continue the transportation process. Along the spiral of Soul are situated the true realms of Soul. The planet, with its Power and Soulparts is like a bus dropping off the Soulparts at the appropriate level of evolving – or realm. Originally when all went as planned with your Universe, Soulparts travelling in a certain planet were all discharged together and then they evolved to the apex together – able to enjoy each other's company whilst doing this.

So the Soulparts grow in understanding, carrying with them the radiance that is Power – the radiance that you see to a very small degree upon your moon today. This radiance is so different to the light you know of. But even this Power, this radiance, is dull in comparison with the Essence I give to Souls. I make the Essence for Souls from the Power that they create. This Essence I give to Souls is brighter than the brightest light that you know of. Brighter than a million suns.

With the constant production of Power in the way I have mentioned, a Soul increases in size and strength. There comes a point where enough Power has been generated and the way of the Universe can continue without need of an Earth or Soulparts upon that Earth. When this point is reached the Soul is said to be fulfilled. You can compare it with the lighting of a coal fire. Heat is needed at first to cause the coal to glow, but once the coal starts to burn then the original heating source can be taken away.

You of man burn away your livelihood. You burn away

what is needed by your Soul. I mince no words on this score, for it is vital that you realise what you do.

All along the line man uses what he has no right to use. He takes at all stages the natural fuels from the Earth – the peat, the coal, the oil, the gas. So stupid it is to act so cruelly to yourselves – for it is only your Soul that you ruin. After all you *are* your Soul – you are this great being, but never for one minute consider it to be so.

Too long has man fooled around with his religious rules of society, twisting and mis-using what his voice tells him, through greed of self. He at present would rather waste his thoughts and the Power which is his own life-line – his own existence.

Such comfort and understanding await his minds awakening. In a matter of a few years – if man placed his output into the ground in a nice way – then the Earth would warm ... and warm ... and warm. No need then to burn what is in the ground at present. In any case, this would only last out for say, no longer than the lifetime of his children. Yes, if man used his output correctly, in say, two or so years you would see a noticeable change – a change that would increase rapidly over the following years. You would then see the summers becoming noticeably longer, and the winters shortening. Days would start to be longer and nights shorter. All would become lighter and warmer. The lands now parched by the sun would become milder also. All these things and more – much much more – *will* occur, but only if man cares enough to act in the way of Powering his Soul.

I tell you just a small fraction of the wonders that await you in the coming years.

The Earth will become a nice place to live upon – without need to burn to have light and heat. Your soils will become fertile and produce food in abundance. New and better ways of living will be shown to you – ways so simple, so ingenious. But all these wonders will have to be earned. Man will have to show his worth before Soul acts. All now must be earned.

Soul does not expect you to go without light or warmth, and with the way things are at present you can only use the ways of fuel that are available to you. Yet there is a better way which you can start upon. You can each start on the way of securing a warm and cosy future for your children and their children. They – I am sure that you will agree – deserve to have as good a chance as you can give them. This Earth at present is in a bad way. It needs the caring that you can give to it.

Over the ages of time of this Universe your Soul has endeavoured to allow you to choose right and wrong. But you are only aware of wrong. Even wrong has a right way to act, and a wrong way to act out the wrong. You could say that man has perfected a technique of how to put to rights his way in the sense of wrong.

Look around you and see how man's life at present is spent in trying to correct what *he* thinks is wrong. But how can he possibly put to rights when he knows no other way save wrong? This constant struggle causes such violence and disharmony all over the world.

Man ruins the plants, the lives of animals and his own Earth in a vain attempt to make nature fit into *his* way of things. Rather he should change himself so as to be natural and at harmony with all. He devises laws and customs to try to force others to do what he wants. Religions and societies set certain so-called moral and social standards, which are supposed to dictate what is right and what is wrong. Right being the ways which conform to society and religion, and wrong being the ways which do not.

In one society for example, it may be deemed right to eat the carcasses of certain animals. – In another it may not. In one it might be quite normal and acceptable to wear no clothing. – In another it may not. In one country or religion it may be the law to have only one wife, in another it may be permissible to have more. And so it goes on – man in one society thinking that his rules and standards are right and just, yet the same rules in another society are considered quite wrong. A large majority may adopt certain values, but that does not make them right.

Not only does man assume what is right and what is wrong, but he also tries to force others into following these adopted values. He goes to great lengths to influence others and defend what he imagines to be right and wrong – without even attempting to examine where his own ideas stem from. Many consider it is right to kill bird, animal and insect in order to keep certain crops of food for man. Yet they fail to consider if the crops in question were intended for human consumption – or whether they are in fact the food provided specifically for the creatures that they kill. Many people consider that it is right that children should be forced to attend school – but they do not realise that in Soul each has the knowledge of the whole Universe.

Your Soul knows all too well which is the best way for you to live your lives on Earth, yet it does not at any time judge you or force its way upon you. It merely puts its way forward – leaving the choice as to whether or not to use what it sends entirely up to you.

How futile it is then for you to say what is right or what is wrong – or what is good or what is bad – without knowing the purpose of things upon this Earth. Right and wrong, good and bad, are merely words which society uses to show how a person or persons should or should not act according to the laws of that society. Man on Earth has the choice between fulfilling his purpose in life, or not. No more, no less. Ways of value – caring, gentleness and respect – enhance that purpose. Selfish and intolerant ways – the ways of lesser value – detract from that purpose.

Each one's task is different, but all have the same end in view so to speak. Each task completed, enables the Soul of this Universe to be fulfilled and the Soulparts to evolve. Too often nowadays, man thinks that if you live in a certain way – *all* should live that way too. But this is so wrong, for one person's task on Earth may be so very different from anothers. So only by first knowing – and then following – your own purpose in life, can you begin to truly help another without encroaching upon his or her task. That way you allow their Soul – your Soul – to give what is best for them. Act in accordance with your purpose and you bring peace and harmony of Soul to yourself and those around.

What peace and harmony awaits all mankind. What happy companionship and cosy living. But only when he *himself* cares to make it so. Only when he cares enough to make *himself* right – instead of right, within the wrong.

Only when he changes the kindness to caring, the helpful ways to the purposeful ways, the sympathy to guiding strength and the guessing to knowing beyond all possible doubt – only then will he be truth. But truth can be, and should be, his by right. So simple. So easy to achieve. You are as you are to fulfil a purpose for Soul, so by fulfilling that purpose you have a fulfilled life in return. Be fulfilled – fill your own lives and the lives of others to fullness – fullness of understanding and happiness and purpose.

I now place for your consideration a story. A story of many parts and many ages. It is the story of a Soul.

It was to be a wondrous place. A shining orb which heralded a beginning – a birth – a new start. It was as a precious jewel newly glowing with the light of life. I looked upon this place with such joy – the joy of a mother first seeing her new born. It held out its arms to me, and I came to guide and cherish this new born Soul – sending many Soulparts from neighbouring Universes to nurse and tend this place so that all would start off in a good way.

The Soul was content. It placed a cloak of caring around the mighty Soulparts as they came to start their task – a task of bearing and teaching the Soul's new beings. The Soulparts came with such grace and wisdom, taking the shape of the Soul's new beings for one lifetime. They did not come as babes, but as adults ready to propogate the new land.

They were mighty of stature – far taller and steadier than man upon this Earth at present – so strong of body and mind. Such caring they had for the place where they lived – caring of all that was in the land, using all in a good way, and enjoying to the full what was provided for the workings of the machine that is the cocoon. The mighty ones showed by example what value there is in caring, teaching their off-spring so caringly and gently of the wisdom that was the Soul.

Such hopes we had. Such hopes that this would be a garden of gardens – a place where Soulparts could grow to the highest realms of Soul.

You must understand that this place was so different to what you imagine – not a garden as you know vegetation and your Earth today. There is no comparison.

It was Soul in every way. A home. So harmonious and warming. Such variety – such an interesting place. The colours were so brilliant, so crisp and deep – even with the newness. Yet all was so restful and comforting to the senses. The land rolled gently along to the horizon, with no buildings. – no obstacles to block the natural beauty of the countryside. And the cloudless sky was so light and warming, constantly. It was daytime *all* the time. No Sun – no need for a sun when the whole sky showered the land with a gentle light. A light not hurtful nor tiring to the eyes, but restful and of the most silvery golden radiance.

In the constant light and warmth there was no need for shelter of any kind. The earth was so springy and soft, so pliable under foot. It was so comfy to lie and sit upon. It had such a fine covering – not grass as you know of it – but a covering of vegetation as a warm fluffy carpet. A carpet which could be stripped back to reveal light fine soil. A rich soft soil, not dirty or hard, but clean and fresh. For the beings placed the Output from the cocoon into it – sustaining it, nourishing it. No mountains nor seas nor lakes in this place, all was moist and fertile.

Vegetation was lush and food plentiful. In this place of no seasons, bushes and shrubs were speckled in profusion over the countryside, and each one bore succulent fruits constantly. The fruits were so delicious and nourishing that just one satisfied the cocoon for many hours, providing enough juices within them so that no liquid intake was required. There were no trees – no need for them – and all food was in easy reach. The fragrance of the fruits and their blossoms drifted on the gentle breezes making the fresh air even more delicious to taste and breathe.

It was a place of great peace and happiness. It was so comforting, so enjoyable. It was paradise.

It was your Earth.

The Soul's new beings came, gentle as their soft golden brown skins, gentle as the warmth of their sparkling eyes. Yet as sure as their words and actions. Man walked with grace then. Grace of movement and grace of thought. He might be in a group or he might be alone – it mattered not. For he was free in all ways to do what he wished and say what he wished. Such beauty of contour, so carefree of manner. Man saw all the beauty around him. He stopped, looked at and understood the skies and the earth, he had time to watch many things for he was in no hurry. He had a whole lifetime. He had his Soul.

Man respected all that he came across – the Earth and all the beings upon it. He was at peace – contented with what his Soul placed before him. He was all-knowing and all-seeing. He listened to his Soul.

The land was so drab to the wonders which he saw in thought. For man in those times, some five million years ago, was truly inspired. Not just a few of man here and there, but *all* of man. Each one knowing themselves and their Universe intimately.

You must understand that in the beginnings of this Earth things were so different to now, and man then had a completely different pattern of thought – completely alien to the ways you experience at present. Compare it if you will with the animals that you see about you. Their pattern is so different and non-understandable to man. Like their communication by movement of limbs, face, eyes etc., their ways of showing caring. Realise that when I speak of times past, it is necessary to be put to you in the pattern of thought that you at present are aware of.

Time also was so different to what it is now. Man's whole life was crammed full of happiness and inspiration, and as now when you are enjoying yourself, things just flashed by. Because man *lived* his intended purpose, only a short stay of earning upon Earth was required – much shorter than is the case today. And with such an interest packed life, the lifetime on Earth appeared like a drop in an ocean of time.

After a lifetime upon this Earth the mighty ones from outside this Universe returned homewards, leaving man to carry on Powering his Soul. They left man in a good way, with each one trusting the next because all trusted their own Soul. The example of caring was passed on down to their off-spring and so on. In fact, such was the calibre of the early ones that man learned from them how to manipulate thought to a high degree – being able to cut and mould substance as though it was not there.

Man in those times was such a great being, so caring of all, so happy in all that he did – spreading that happiness to others. He was natural – as his Soul in so many ways.

CHAPTER SIX

A million years passed after the start of your Earth and all
during that time man fulfilled his task for Soul. The Earth
turned quickly, steadily – as did the whole Universe. And
with the turning came a stability in mind and in actions.
Like a top which quickly spins. It is stable – but let the
top slow down and it starts to waver and wobble. Man also
felt the effects of this spinning. No, he did not become dizzy,
rather he was so solid in his pattern of thought – so clear
cut. After all it is only when you stop spinning that you feel
dizzy. He was solid of movement – not jerky and confused
as today. In this first civilisation of man, each could run,
jump, see, hear and sense far greater distances than man of
today. In those days you could stand say, a long stick upon
its end, and it would take far longer to topple over than if
you did the same nowadays.

The Earth during the first civilisation, was nearly three
times the size of the Earth today. It was a moist spongy mass
all the way through. There was no rock, for no soil was
compressed. The action of the Earth upon man's output was
much quicker and gentler because of this. Power flowed
through so easily. Just as water enables the body to function
easily without friction within, so the moist Earth was kept
in a good way by man's output – thereby placing the lubri-
cating water substances back into it.

Water is a lubricant which contains several substances
which make it appear almost invisible. It is a lubricant for the
way of the Earth and the cocoon, and is able to dissolve
(shall I say) into many substances, changing its own property
and the property of the substance. Substances do not dissolve
into water – water dissolves into them.

Water as you now see it – in rain, ponds and oceans, was not present in any way during the first civilisation of this Earth. Then the water in the soil bonded together with the soil – so different to now, where the sandy unnourished soils fail to contain the moisture within themselves. The moist way of the Earth in the early days lubricated the way of Gas into the atmosphere, making the release cooler and less violent. Man then used the cocoon correctly, and by this processing of soil through the cocoon, bonded the water into the soil – the only way that this bonding can take place.

Time gently passed for man and all was good until one point in time – some four or so million years ago – when a man took a woman to himself in greed. Not so much in the way of physically forcing her, but in the way of wanting the attention of the other so that no one else could enjoy her company – wanting no others to possess her. This way of owning gradually spread to others – slowly at first, but the rot had set in. This small way of greed – possession, was the beginning of the end for Soul-man. This greed led to dissatisfaction and that to more greed.

Whereas before all had been provided in every way, now there was a wanting of more – all that was placed his way previously, but more – and more, and more. The greed gave rise to jealousies and then to intolerance, and then to a whole gamut of other emotions. Understand that this change did not occur overnight so to speak. No, it took many many years to build up in first one person, then the next, then another, then the children and so on – the niggles becoming concerns and the concerns becoming full blown emotions.

During this turning away from his Soul man was sent many senses to warn him of his erring way. For then he knew full well what he did and was well able if he wished, to turn back to the better way of value.

A special warning sense was sent to him by his Soul that would cause him to regret the way that he had taken. This sense was loneliness – not loneliness as you speak of loneliness today, for that is merely self-pity. This loneliness was an aching inside (not physically) but a deep needing to find yourself fully – to find your purpose and your destiny. The loneliness made the seeking of Truth so important. You could compare it with the loss of not knowing the meaning for your life on Earth.

Many used this sense of loneliness to return once again on the way of a fulfilled life. But many did not. And it was through these that the way of emotion and non-understanding started upon this Earth. For the emotions then caused man to turn even further from the way of Soul value.

Emotions are as a distortion to clear thinking. They block off Soul value by twisting and distorting even the most clear cut and caring thought. Emotions cause man to live his life in such an unaware and unsatisfying way. Like driving a car with a dirty windscreen – the covering of dirt blocks off all clarity. Emotions are so destructive and purely selfish – all emotions:– anger, hatred, sympathy, embarrassment, arrogance, humour, pity, confusion, intolerance, fear, concern, deviousness, and a multitude of others. In one way or another they cause the emotional one to think only of self – how self is progressing, how self will appear to others, how the way of self is thought better than any other, what is in it for self, and so on. Self. Self. Self. Never a thought for others – that is, unless the way of another can be used for self.

Emotions distort truth and reality, and far from a person controlling the emotion – the habitial indoctrinated way of emotion in fact controls him. Rather like an alcoholic or a drug addict. – Though the drugs are harmful to the body, an addict (by habit) chooses to take the hurt to self, treasuring it as something valuable – something necessary. Even saying that the hurt *is* his – *is* his own personality or individuality. Emotions rule to such an extent that they are considered quite normal ways of being, today. Normal maybe – but never natural!

Only by turning his attentions towards Soul and his purpose

on Earth, can man rid himself of even one emotion. Only by considering a way regardless of self can he overcome selfishness. But first of all the emotional one must care to be a better person. And being a better person means looking at, and admitting to yourself, how you are. It means examining your old values in the light of new ideas – being open minded to much better ways. It means being prepared to change if necessary. It means caring to look at the bad points and replace them with the good points. *Then* caring enough to put the better ways – the value ways – *into practice*.

There is a plant whose flowers are so beautiful, so white and fragrant. This plant twists itself around other plants, choking them, blocking out more and more light, strangling the very life from them ... but you could just look at the flowers. I care to speak to you now of one particular emotion, that of frustration.

Frustration is not using the natural thoughts and impressions that Soul sends. By natural I mean those which are not influenced by selfish wanting. For example, a thought of sex may come – not because there is constant lusting for such a way, but because the way of the cocoon requires it. Not to use such a thought would mean that you felt, say in a sexy way, yet denied yourself the way of fulfilling the thought.

By man's indoctrinations, inhibitions build up within man and it is these inhibitions that cause him not to use certain "immoral", "unnatural" or "wrong" ways – as *he* thinks. The indoctrinations are so complete that when the frustrations come, the habitual ways are never questioned and so the source of the frustration is never found.

If man used all that came *caringly*, then he would give himself the chance of realising, then overcoming the inhibitions or indoctrinations.

For example. Say a thought came of sex with another. Then if that was used caringly, by mentioning the thought to the other and allowing the other free choice, that would be overcoming the taboos and embarrassments. If a thought came to relieve the body in the way of sex, when there was no other person available, then that could be used in the way of masturbation as man calls it – thereby overcoming the taboos of this natural way.

By using the thoughts *caringly*, regardless of man's taboos, you never become frustrated and all is calm within. You could of course be more afraid of what others think, instead of using the thought caringly.

Realise that in many cases, the way of the cocoon has certain requirements – to ignore or try to push away such requirements brings damage to mind and body to a lesser or greater degree.

Only by using your thoughts as they arrive – caringly – can you be free. For freedom is in the mind – freedom to express what comes naturally – caringly. By using all as it comes, without the selfish distortion of emotion and indoctrination, you *are* free. And by using your thoughts in this way you are so natural – expressing how you are in reality – expressing peace and contentment of Soul.

Such is the way of being truthful:– saying if you are resentful of another, saying if you require the way of sex with another, saying if you have made a mistake, or saying that you disagree. But saying all gently, respectfully and caringly – that is most important. By being truthful and caring at all times you *are free* – in all ways. Free from worries, free from frustrations and emotions. Free to be naturally calm, free to make your own discoveries and your own mistakes, free to be an open book.

I, along with my scribe, open myself to you in all ways. I would not be truth if I did otherwise. In truth I place before you a book. As you open this book, open also yourselves. Open yourselves to a new way, Truth – a new way, Soul.

* * * * *

Upon the Earth today snow falls, but not *because* it is cold. It falls to lessen the effect of the coldness on the soil and vegetation. It is as a blanket sent by Soul to keep the Earth below in a warm way. Notice how grass and plants grow – and continue to grow when snow is upon the ground. The ground is always warmer after the snow has fallen.

Man thinks that the cold *causes* the snow. Rather, it is sent to prevent the damage that the cold causes. What better insulation in times when the atmosphere is cold, than a layer which allows much light through it yet keeps the heat substances within the Earth.

Snow contains a differing substance from water – yet it goes back into what appears to be water. But look closely at the way of snow and you will see, that when it melts, it is slightly – ever so slightly – gritty. It can be taken into the cocoon as refreshment liquid and it easily blends itself into the way the water is, but it has no properties of water – yet man insists that it has.

Now it is time for much knowledge to come your way – a little at a time, for it is better that way – that way teaches patience also. Ice and snow are a combination of similar substances, yet each are a little different in being than the other.

Now Ice is a strange commodity. So strange in fact that man requires experimental stations to be placed upon it – places where he drills holes in it, melts it, even causes it to surround his way of life. These men and women who search into its ways are numbed – numbed by the preserving quality that it has – Ice is devoid of substances that are called by man "salt", and snow also is in part devoid of this commodity. Those who are interested in the ways of these matters are puzzled at the way it hides so much, so well.

What does it hide? What lies beneath the seemingly harsh and unyielding cover?

It hides value. Land. Rich fertile land waiting to come forth for the use of man. A soil preserved for a time when man deserves the rich bounties that can be obtained from it. But to look now at the so called "poles" of the Earth – the frozen wastes – you would imagine barrenness below. But there is warmth. There is land so soft and pliable waiting to burst forth for the deserving ones.

I look upon the Earth and see another covering – one equally as cold and uninviting. But this time the covering surrounds man himself. I see a harsh covering, but great warmth within. Such warmth that could easily be turned to removing the outer covering. Warmth that could spread to all of mankind so that each could move about without the burden around. The covering that I speak of is not Ice nor clothing of any kind. It is a way of thought – a way of acting and living that is unnatural to the one that it surrounds. It is the way of emotion. Ways which prevent the caring and gentle ways (the natural ways) from shining forth to warm the way ahead. I see a covering of violence, selfishness, uncaring. But I see underneath each of man, one so caring of all on this Earth – one who can give great comfort and understanding to those around.

Ice covers such beauty. It does indeed.

When the Soul of this Earth saw how things were with man and his emotions, it folded in the way of that first civilisation, leaving just a few of man – those who had earned the right – to stay and start off in a new and better way. So the second civilisation of man began.

But the seed of emotion still remained – so deeply ingrained had it become. And so slowly but surely throughout the next million years it once again began to grow. Man once again started to neglect his Earth and his fellow man for the greed of self. Even at the beginning of this civilisation Soul sent to this Earth other mighty Soulparts from other Universes, so that man could learn from their example. They came and assisted – but only assisted – in the way of maintaining the correct functioning of the Earth. They could not – unlike man – help in fulfilling the Soul. *That* task had to be done by man himself. The new beings came in the shape that you call "birds".

When the birds were originally introduced they were able

to live naturally, in a way different than you know today – spending the majority of their lives on the wing and only requiring to land to give birth. With the introduction of birds came the way of insects. These originally as food for the birds, but later when the Earth hardened through man's neglect, other insects were introduced to break up the soils and chew upon the rotting leaves and vegetation.

But man continued to ignore his task upon Earth, and to choose the way of selfish emotions. So other Soulparts came to this Earth in the form of animals, when it was seen that all would come to a standstill without their help. You must realise that even with the birds, the way of the Earth gradually deteriorated during the second civilisation, and it was only towards the end that animals were introduced. Even though more and more of man began to ignore the way of Soul value, the earth was in those times still soft enough for the animals to dig with hooves or claws.

The clawed variety inhabited the softer soil areas, and the hooved varieties inhabiting the harder areas neglected by man. Even nowadays this way is indicated – with the clawed varieties needing to occupy the softer lands which man ravaged, they have had greater contact with the greed and viciousness of man. Notice how the clawed varieties of animals are on the whole more vicious, and how man with his ways has driven them out of their natural habitat, teaching them to eat their fellow beings.

Once again all went from bad to worse. And once again another civilisation of man had to be ended.

You must understand that to fold in a civilisation is a saddening time for a Soul, and it is only undertaken when absolutely necessary. To the Soul, it is like tearing yourself inside out so to speak. It is an upheaval of the whole Earth. Mountains turning over like sods of earth after a plough. The sound is deafening – like a constant thundering but much, much louder. The whole Earth is literally split assunder.

It is a means of quickly and painlessly taking Soulparts

homewards. And only a few remain afterwards, scattered about the upturned face of the Earth – a few chosen ones strong in the way of Soul caring – those say, in transit above and away from the mangling and folding below – or those on a part of the Earth separated from the main movements. In time these few dotted about the Earth appear, looking and looking for other survivors of the last civilisation.

Yet another two civilisations came and went in much the same way as the ones previously. Even though many, many times in each civilisation messengers were sent from outside of this Universe to take on the shape of man and bring him back once again to the way of value. At *all* – I repeat *all* – the times when the way of emotion came to the fore, such messengers came. Even at the beginnings of man taking the way of self they came, trying to warn man of the consequences of such a way. But out of all the attempts made to assist man over the past five million years, none were put into fruition for Soul – all failed, even though some came so near to success. The seed of emotion is so difficult to remove.

I speak to you now of one such messenger who came to your Earth a mere fifty-six thousand years ago. He came to a land vast in area – extending over the parts you now know of as the Pacific Ocean. This vast land was known as Lemuria, and in the time that I speak of it had virtually been turned to sand and dust by man's neglect of his soil over the centuries. Time and time again throughout the days of Lemuria, messengers had come to speak my words. But all were ignored. And so, over the years, Lemuria had become such a barren and dry place. Even today this can be seen to be so, merely by looking at the sandy, rocky sea-bed of the Pacific. No rivers or tides could cover such a large expanse, for their affects are only felt close inshore or on the surface of the oceans – *not* on the sea-bed.

This age was one of constant warring, in a continent of so much savagery, man against man. None cared in any way for the next – all was such greed and cruelty – greed in the way of ownership of land and people, rather than gold and jewels. Each wanted power and more power over others. It was under such conditions that a saviour came to this Earth. Came just as any of man – born of a family, growing in body form from babe to youngster to adult. The saviour's name was Youru.

Very early on in life he became aware of the way of life around him. He saw all too clearly the extreme tenseness and turmoil of the mind of man. He saw how none trusted the next – always suspecting, always judging – always in fear of their very lives. For life in those times was cheap indeed.

In his younger days Youru was taken to a place of entertainment, where – in front of a cheering, bloodthirsty crowd – men, women and children were killed and tortured. And that was merely an everyday occurrence. Nothing compared with the atrocities perpetrated upon, whom you might now term, "enemies of the state". For the way of rule in those times was by pompous ones who resided in exotic buildings, and dressed in highly decorative long flowing gowns. Merely by the flick of a wrist the ruling ones could end a life – so easily, no fuss. They and their bullies below them, had at their disposal such sophisticated ways of travel and weaponry. Weapons such as those which melted away the very bones of the body – but left other tissues unaffected.

Many of those who caused or ordered the use of such weapons, still – even today – pay back by living lives within twisted or malformed bodies. All pay, one way or another.

Youru lived *as* man, *amongst* man, until a point in time when he was in his twenties. Then Soul came to Youru in a form of an awakening – an awakening to who he really was. Amidst all this cruelty, a saviour came forward in caring.

Such a stir he caused in the place where he lived. Word spread and many came for help and guidance – if they came in sincerity, they received it. Youru moved about the land, curing those who wanted to be cured of their diseases and their afflictions. Many courageous ones joined him, but many hated him – for he spoke truth, he spoke of Soul.

But man only wanted *his* way, preferring to put down rather than listen to a better way. So after a few years the saviour along with many of his companions, were captured by the powerful ones. They tortured the saviour to try to make him speak against Soul – but no words did he utter against anyone! He was crippled and mutilated, exhibited to the people and burned alive. They had killed the body, but they could not touch the Soul. No, not in any way.

Many of the saviour's companions were loyal to Soul unto death, and the Soul of the Earth was greatly pleased with many – one you know of already, the one you now call Jesus.

Man had failed to listen, and so once again things worsened with him – until Soul in disgust again closed down into the sea, a land. Lemuria. Little of it remains, and what does is not so useful now, merely a few islands – nothing more.

*   *   *   *   *

A child plays with his friends. He paints or builds, models or whatever – later when he is a little older, he might build himself a shelter or make a temporary home out of a cave or over-hanging rock. He might cook himself some food on a fire, and with his still clumsy hands make decorations for his playhouse. It is all great fun to be away from the parents and to be catering for himself and his friends.

Now who would imagine that these antics – many years later – would be studied by the most educated of experts, and even have a branch of science named after it? Well, it occurred. For many years ago, children – like today – played in caves and shelters. And sometimes the children painted on the roof and walls, sometimes making wood and clay utensils for eating and storage. But nowadays many many such items are taken to show "how primitive man has been in the past". Of course it suits man's idea to think that he has advanced, and so he believes such talk. But to look at man today with his wars, with his ways of hammering and bashing at things, with his ways of bruising muscles and painting the body, it would seem to an onlooker that he in fact is the cave man. Many even live in shelters of soil or rock!

Many articles found in children's dwellings which cannot be seen to have a specific purpose, are taken to be religious symbols or deities. An easy way out if ever there was one.

Never do any consider that the findings could just be the doodlings of small children:– children's games, dolls or merely abstract decorations like many household objects of today.

You talk of ice-ages, iron-ages, cave man, evolution – all nonsense, all untrue. Man looks at the animals and birds and because some of their shapes are similar he presumes that they evolved from one source. Just a wild assumption – and then without even knowing their purpose. You are told wild stories of monsters and dinosaurs by ones who gather together a conglomeration of animal bones – ones who pick and choose the bones to suit their ideas – then guess a convenient body shape from the fragments they have managed to fit together. Such untruths they tell – even using and teaching methods of dating, which show roadside grass to be thousands of years old!

Then you have those who look at the Earth with the eyes of today and imagine that it has always been as today – that rivers have flowed, that wind has blown and rain has fallen. Rivers have only formed because the soil has become so hard and moistureless. Rain is provided especially to moisten the land and feed these rivers. Mountains have been formed through upheaval and the shrinking of the Earth like a dried fruit. Trees have been introduced so that wind can act upon them and turn the Earth – turn it so slowly, when it should be spinning around so fast, so surely.

Many look at the soil and rock of the Earth and say that it is of differing ages. Yet I say that rock is soil – all the same age, but in differing states of goodness.

Others look at the heavens for clues into their past, when all could be known by listening to their thoughts. They search the skies for clues. But the skies now change and things are not as they have expected. Stars disappear and move about. Cameras and measuring instruments fail to detect what should be there, but isn't! In the years to come many changes will occur in the heavens, in the climates, in the passage of time. So it is far better that these ones speak out of the changes that they have seen, instead of quietly hoping that things will revert back to "normal."

But many speak their minds harshly, uncaringly, with the intention of doing the other down, and with no idea of helping the other in any way. That is not how man should be, in such cases it would be better to be truthful, admitting to yourselves and others that you have allowed yourself to be uncaring of others, and in many cases admitting to being so selfish as to want to force your way upon others. Having done this, a caring one who sought Truth would be able to overcome the intolerances by considering the *true reason* for such disrespectful behaviour as keeping truth from others.

You are as I in Soul. Consider now the way of this Earth. It turns. But how does it turn, how does it move? Your Earth at present is barely turning – being dragged along by the thought of your own Soul in the form of winds. It rotates ... or does it? It would seem that it would rotate about what is known as an axis. But this is not as you imagine, for though the Earth turns it does not have an axis. You could imagine it to be like the turning of a ball in two directions at once. Hence you have the reason for variation in what you call magnetic north pole and true north pole.

Each morning you see the sun-disc rising into the sky and in the evening you see it setting – imagining that the Earth goes round the sun, yet I say that it does not. No more does it do this than the sun goes round the Earth. No, you are – together with the stars and the planets – at the base of your Universe, hanging like a pendulum below the disc (not sphere) that is the sun.

You are as I in Soul, and you too can know of and understand much more if you care to do so. If you care to understand your purpose on Earth, care to understand yourself. Realise that understanding has to be earned, and here I do mean understanding – not merely the gathering of knowledge – but understanding of the knowledge gained.

Understanding is a strange thing – a feeling that gives great confidence and comfort. Even more so when it is understanding your true self. Understanding is realising (or seeing) all the ways in which the knowledge gained can be applied. It is to fully appreciate the application of that knowledge. To know knowledge you must understand. It is rather like looking through a telescope at a night sky and just seeing an array of white dots. When with understanding, you would know their beauty, their purpose and their application to your own purpose.

Have your ever realised a point of understanding? Perhaps you have in relation to your life at present. It is a time when things click into place, when you suddenly know how to use the knowledge in the best way. It might be solving a problem at work or in the home. It might be in reading part of this book.

Understanding is a wonderful thing. Such a nice feeling there is, so amazing, so comforting. There is a feeling of having done something worthwhile, something that has been earned through one way or another.

This is what your Soul holds out to you – understanding. A life of understanding upon understanding. A life unfolding so many new aspects as you go along.

Have you noticed that to be able to understand anything, you have had to be caring of it in some way? It is so. You must, at one time or another, place yourself in a way of seeking to care. You must *care* to understand. True understanding complements itself – each aspect of understanding complements other aspects. This is understanding of your Soul. Little by little, new and unusual aspects open out to you and the understanding of each aspect adds to the overall understanding. Rather like building a jig-saw puzzle. Each piece is taken and looked at from all angles then is put into the picture. As more pieces are added you begin to see the overall picture, until finally the picture is complete and you are as your Soul in understanding.

Each piece fits.

Every piece is used in the picture – nothing is left out.

CHAPTER SEVEN

Cold. You say that you have a cold. Yet you do not know what it is or why it occurs.

A cold is a means of clearing the body. For it rids the body of the pollution and dross of man that has gathered in the passages of the eyes, ears, nose, sinuses, throat and chest. It is caused – not by an infection or germ as man thinks – but by a changing of the substance in the atmosphere. You see, it is necessary with the way things are at present, for substances required in the atmosphere to be fed to this Earth from other Souls. And the effects of this replenishing process upon man vary from time to time and from place to place – depending on the type and strength of the substances introduced. Also, different people react in different ways to this change, according to the state of their bodies and the amount of dross that has gathered within. One person could have a cold some days after another, and it need not be of the same severity that the one before experienced.

Colds are not necessary if a child at birth is allowed to cry its fill. For it is in this crying that the mucus from the sac within the womb is cleared out from the passages. If this mucus is not removed at birth it adheres to the passage-ways, remaining there for the rest of that person's life. And no matter how much crying is done in later years the damage is already done.

Not only does this mucus collect the pollution of man but it also prevents the person – right from the start – from receiving the thoughts of his Soul in a good way. The remaining mucus hinders the transfer of thought from the Soul to the receiving set or brain, as it travels through the body passages. If the child was allowed to cry at birth, then the thoughts would be unhindered and there would be no mucus to which the dross could adhere.

As it is, man at present has colds. His eyes water and his nose runs, he coughs and he sneezes. It may even be necessary to clear out the dross adhering to the mucus by blowing the nose. Even on days when man says that he does not have a cold, the substance of the air is changing constantly. This is apparent at the times when the body had been relatively still in movement. Times say, during slumbers, when the body is without fluid intake for several hours and the dross substances have had time to set. I am sure that you all will have noticed how, after sleeping, dross collects in the corners of the eyes, in the chest and throat, as a tacky layer within the mouth, even as wax within the ears.

It is worth mentioning at this point that many cold symptoms (soreness of eyes, headaches and general stuffiness and dryness within) are in fact due to the lack of water intake into the body, or lack of salt intake. Water – not oils – being a lubricant for the body, and salt being a cleanser and preserver. Even without a cold, lack of one of these two substances causes similar symptoms – so it is important not to neglect *both* ways.

You must realise that not only does man suffer from colds because of the encroachment early in life – he suffers from many illnesses also. Such things as wheezes, catarrh, coughs and other ailments of the chest and throat. He suffers from headaches, ear aches, sinus troubles, soreness and damage to eyes and ears and nose – even snoring and what is known as "hay-fever"!

So think on my words the next time that you have such an illness or cold. Would you like to be the one to bring these things upon another? Would you like to be the cause of hindering a person from receiving the thoughts from their Soul? You would be – if you prevented a child from crying its fill at birth!

Now the passage ways of the eyes, ears, nose, throat etc.,

are connected to a sac which man calls the thyroid. The sac in its correct function secretes a way of saline through ducts into the passage ways. This is a very weak form of salt solution – as when the eyes water the tear ducts put out this saline, and it tastes and *is* salty – cleansing all as it goes. Only when the sac is empty of saline does the dross quickly build up. Because the substances of the atmosphere are moving and changing rapidly by the way of breathing, the build-up of dross – whether it be in a light or heavy way, depends upon the quantity of saline within the sac.

Even the ears are connected to the sac, and when there is no salt in the sac, too much wax forms in the ears. Notice how, if you solidify the dross of the nose by driving off the water, you obtain the same as the so-called wax of the eardrum.

The substances of the air around you are not as you imagine. They are in fact solid and rasp against the nostril, causing at times a tickle which can work up to a sneeze. It is good to sneeze, for that helps to clear the small areas within the tubes. You could liken it to a sudden movement, a jolting – of the slow moving air lodged in the cavities.

Notice how stuffy and dry a room could become through the burning of coal, oil or gas. This is because the way of heat solidifies the substances of the air into heavy dross, although it does not appear to be so. This heavy dross gathers, often blocking the channels within. The way of natural gas (as you call it) is better than that of the air – not in the way of breathing but because it is lighter in texture.

In order to allow the cleansing substances to do their task, man should not try to restrict the flow of air into and out of the passages. At present he does this by such ways as, stifling the coughs and sneezes that his Soul gives to move the dross, and by wearing tight clothing which restricts his breathing.

Yet when no saline is available to clear out the passages constantly the dross of the atmosphere clings to the walls. This quickly works its way into what looks like the pus of a sore. Man then can relieve the way of it by blowing it down the nostrils safely away from the body.

But he can also let the pus slide down his throat into the way of the stomach, where it contaminates the intake. This contamination then has to be worked upon by the juices of the stomach or the whole system of the cocoon would suffer detrimental blockage. Salt is necessary to cleanse such dross from the system. Yet even when the pus is taken into the stomach it cannot be fully worked upon, and the part that clogs goes into the intestines. You will have noticed – particularly after a bout of influenza – that the stools when they come are hard and with a coating of mucus on them at times.

When drugs have been used, the anti-biotics (as they are termed) clog the movement of the stools even more so, and the dross then starts a way of its own, it comes out alone as a stool would. This way causes haemorrhoids to start.

Now salt has a curious property of causing many substances to become liquid, or mobile. This is the case with the dross which collects within the passage ways for thought. To release any build-up that may occur, salt should be applied. So whenever you find that there is discomfort, you should sniff a little dry salt up the nose – as you would do snuff. This is very effective and quickly releases the pus outwards. If you find yourself only starting to become blocked in some way, you could then take a less drastic step. A small amount of water with a small amount of salt, say the taste similar to tears, should be taken daily. This simple way cleanses the pipes, and can be continued without damage, preventing dross from ever gathering within the body of man.

No wonder many people in the past have found a little relief from working a salt solution around the throat area. They would however, have benefitted more by swallowing the solution – thereby allowing it to cleanse more of the passage ways and be collected in the sac.

Water also is necessary to lubricate the way of the body and if one has insufficient fluid, the sac then goes solid and dries up.

A way was introduced some years ago upon those who sailed the oceans. Just like the mis-conception that lack of fresh fruit caused scurvy (when in fact the roe of poorly cleansed fish caused the illness) – so the way of iodine was introduced into salt, to relieve inflamation of the thyroid, as they then thought. Through the sailors taking such treated salt, they cured themselves of the inflamation, but it was not the fact that they took iodine into the body that cured them – it was the fact that they took more *salt* into the body. Simply that.

Yet even nowadays we see the way of iodine used so widely as a cleanser of the body – when it is no use to man's body in any way whatsoever! Iodine is provided for the benefit of the fish in the oceans.

Merely by taking in salt in the way that I have directed, man can cure *all* illnesses of the sac which man calls the thyroid.

Salt is a most marvellous substance – a cleanser for the body of man, and the way of the Earth. The only substance that dissolves itself into the way of what you know of as water, disappearing as it does so. Yet it can under certain circumstances re-appear as its original way. It leaves the way of the water in the ground when warmth of the atmosphere dries it out.

In the early days of this Earth there was salt all the way through it, and so the food of man contained all that was required in this way. Because of the abundance of salt throughout the Earth the Power left the Earth in a good way – unlike now when it is necessary for the outer rim of the atmosphere to contain salt. At the outer rim of the atmosphere, salt cleanses the outgoing gases, yet allows the way of the incoming dross to come through unaffected.

Another way of the body I am now going to relate to you. Now I bring to your notice a way of the cocoon that has man baffled. The way of the outer skin. It requires a way of mine – Malgum.

The cocoon is substance through and through and it is without doubt outside of what man is in reality. For man in reality can be any shape that he cares to be – but preferring to be his original self. Spiritualists would have you believe that you and others can roam freely about the earth in the form of a spirit – if this was how Soulparts behaved, then they could do so, but in fact, do not.

Malgum is a way of thought substance, with a special Essence from the Core of Power. It is inserted into all beings as they are prepared for a life on Earth, and is the means of man retaining his shape – instead of mixing into other substances. Malgum determines the shaping, ageing and growth of the body. But I only mention Malgum in passing, for man on Earth would never be able to discover its properties – never intended that he should. Only when he becomes a Soul in his own right will the way be unfolded to him.

The shape of man worries man – it's either too large – too small – too fat – too thin, and so on. Then, there is the matter of colour of skin tissue. That affects him most of all, so now I speak to you of the way of differences of colour, and the respect, or lack of it, towards those differences.

Africa, a country of vast differences – differences in opinion, differences of peoples, and differences in climate and in custom. There is no respect for the differences, no caring for things different.

In Africa – as in many countries of the world today – man fights man. This is no accident, no freak of nature. It was planned that this would occur, in order than man could pay back for all the wrongs that he may have done, in this life and lives previously.

Now is the age of paying back – an age when each being wipes the slate clean, so to speak, ready to evolve further. Ready for the age of enlightenment that dawns.

You see, the way of repayment is necessary for a being to

evolve. And so each being now arranges a life which will remove all the obstacles – all the shackles – which he has gradually built up over lives previously.

A being in order to evolve, first comes to Earth to do a task for its Soul. During the time on earth the being has two ways to go – the value way and the rubbish way. By choosing the value, the being fulfils its task and evolves – never needing to return again to Earth. If the rubbish is chosen then the task is failed and the being encroaches upon others during the life.

Now in Soul, all finish what they set out to do – all is continued until completion, never left half done. So the being who has failed in its first life on Earth arranges another life to overcome the few obstacles that were created by say, encroaching upon others. But then – due to the indocrination of man – the being encroaches further, taking again the way of rubbish. And so it goes on. The being gathering more and more obstacles around itself which prevent it from evolving.

All must be paid back in full. That is the way of Soul. What one does to another *will* be done back to that one in return. So now we see violence and cruelty once again upon this Earth. The Soulpart arranges that to repay, it returns to Earth in various guises. It arranges to be a number of people who can – if they take that way – war against each other. For example, it could choose to be leaders of countries or even the members of an intolerant family. What better way of repayment, than to yourself. But no repayment is necessary when one or more of the parties concerned take the way of Soul value. For then they do all that is asked of them, and Soul would not allow caring ones to suffer in any way – no matter what they have done in the past.

You cannot understand what all is about until you listen to the way of the voice within. If you do not do this, then you take the wrong way, and then you start to judge your fellow man.

The sentence is passed, the mallet falls, and another life is ruined – even ended. But the hand that judges can be the one who in turn, will be judged. It is so always.

Judging is a way of man, a way of thought that Soul sends for man to choose if he wishes. It is, like so many other emotions, an intolerance.

A person chooses – rightly or wrongly – a particular way to go in life. That is fine for that person – they have decided how they are going to live and presumably attempt to remain that way. But then to assume that one person's way is right for another *is* to judge. Really, it is to presume that you know best, when in truth, there could be no understanding there of the other person's purpose in life. To judge a person in this way could (and often does) lead to encroachment upon their purpose.

Another way of judging is to assume. Assume that a person should know better, or assume that certain events have occurred when they have not. You may have noticed this way when such assumptions have been proved to be false. Such situations occur when the information received is second hand – where you are told that this or that occurred or "it happened in this way". Many things which are spoken of in such a way do occur. But you must always remember that what is said, is seen through the eyes of another – and that other person may well be looking through a haze of emotion or indoctrination. So often we hear of vastly differing accounts of the same situation.

There is another very important aspect to consider also. That is the fact that none can know another's thoughts. So you could have a person acting in all good intentions, yet to another the action may seem very uncaring. If you listen to the way of your inner voice you will know without doubt what is Truth, rather than assume as you are apt to do. For Soul knows Truth. Soul knows because it is all – because it sends every thought to every man woman and child upon this Earth.

But who then would judge Soul? Many will, to be sure – many will think that their way is good and right, but would fail to look within themselves.

There is no need for any to judge another. No need whatsoever. Each gets what he deserves – whether it be value or rubbish – whether it be peace of mind or agony of mind – whether it be understanding or ignorance.

The judgement made will be the judgement received. As you think, so you are. Each pays for the judgement of another to lesser or greater degrees. The judging thought leads to a worrying thought and that leads to fear. Those who judge are afraid. It is so. For why would any judge another unless they were afraid that their way might be wrong – that they might be found out for what they are – they are afraid of the consequences of their actions.

Man would say that it is necessary to judge in order that there could be law and order – law yes, but order, no! Law is merely a set of rules that are forced upon one set of people, by another set of people – again encroaching, again thinking that their way is right, but none should encroach upon another by judging.

Justice is judging. It is to presume that another deserves this or that. Yet this cannot be known without knowing another's thoughts or motives. Teachers judge how a life should be lived, indocrinating the child towards the way of the society – leaving little or no free choice for the pupil to disagree with that society. A better way would be to teach each child caring rather than judging. Caring. Caring to allow others to go their own way – to make their own mistakes and their own successes – to allow them free choice. It is having the courage to allow this choice, knowing that by doing so you do not try to persuade nor condemn – knowing that, in many cases, they may cause themselves trouble.

In being open you cannot judge, for then you are open-minded and so respect another's way or point of view. Then you are also open to receive thoughts for the sake of others. That is value. – Caring and understanding.

Remember that all ways are the ways that your Soul sends to you to accept or reject. They can be value or rubbish, but all are ways of Soul and *all* are sent for a reason. In judging any of such ways you then are disrespectful to your own Soul.

> Choose respect not revenge.
> Caring not condemning.
> Understanding rather than judging.

Seek to understand your own thoughts before you even attempt to speak for another. By doing this you can then understand your own purpose, the way of this Earth, the way of man upon this Earth, the way of your own Soul. Judging comes from non-understanding – a failure to appreciate your own and another's task in life.

In ignorance man judges that his sun is a sphere. In ignorance, man judges what is right, and what is wrong. In ignorance, he fails to understand who he really is. In ignorance, he judges what is good and what is bad.

I am. I am Power and Intelligence. I put these words before you, that you may know yourselves. I am Soul – come to your Earth to give myself to mankind – come to Earth in the form of a thought, a thought operating a body. I send the thought of myself to bring to mankind a better way to be. I bring to man the caring of Soul.

I care for you, mankind. I do indeed! I care that you understand your *own* Soul – the source of all your thoughts. I care enough to show you – in a limited way of words – how you are cared for by your own dear Soul.

This is the task which I have set myself. The task *will* be fulfilled – I Soul, say so.

No matter how many ridicule, or turn away from my words, I will still care for you so much – still give my all to you, regardless of self.

I say, you are as I in Soul. And never would I harm one

who is as I. Even if that one did not realise that it is so. Even if that one chose to ignore the way of its own Soul – its own true self.

Soul gives free choice. Always, it gives free choice. That is most important. No forcing nor persuading. No selling or fooling. The decision must always be yours – whether to follow the way pointed out, or not.

With caring we come. With caring we leave. With caring we say how all is, and how all can be.

With caring, you are as I in Soul!

"ORISSOR" ...
is the way for All
Dorothy Fosbrooke

Why cause yourselves to have CANCER, or for
that matter any sickness whatsoever?

Why ponder over the ways of this Universe?
Understand your own Earth and in which Universe
it dwells. Every-one can understand what *all* is about.

I say that you can use substance as well as I can –
whether you believe me or not is for you to decide.

Everyone on Earth should have free choice to
make their own decisions.

NEVER BEYOND UNDERSTANDING

Keith D. Edmunds

You are here on Earth for a definite purpose.
You can understand what that purpose is.

Within these pages is information of many ways –
ways of thoughts and senses, and how your
Universe truly functions as one of many other
Universes.

Past, Present and Future are herein.

Ways of putting the mind at ease. Ways of clearing
once and for all time, from the face of your Earth
the ailments of man.

Make sure you understand the contents, and be
sure to ask if you are in doubt.

THE GOLDEN AGE OF ENLIGHTENMENT - IS HERE

Bill Dawson

One spark can make a forest fire. One spark of pure Truth can set the World alight with Understanding of all things.

What is contained in this book can be that spark, for it brings Wisdom from *outside* of this Universe of yours, to bear on the real-life problems of Mankind.

Knowledge of eradicating *all* the illnesses and disorders of Man, quickly and simply, is contained within.

Illnesses of body and troubles of mind. Knowledge of the World and Universe around you. Knowledge of other Universes and the Beings who inhabit them.

It brings you knowledge of the Aliens who walk among you now, whom you do not recognise – as yet.

The Being from the Core of All Power and Intelligence enlightens you on how to use Pure Thought, and contact your own Higher Intelligence – easily.

But all this is only for those with courage to face the new Age of Enlightenment which is now being kindled.

Are *you* one of them?

INSPIRATION - IS FOR ALL
Bill Dawson

How was this Universe formed? What lies outside of this Universe? What is your true purpose on Earth? Where did you come from before you began life on Earth? What other kinds of Beings exist outside of this World, this Universe?

. What kind of a Man was Jesus? And was he anti-religious? Is it true that highly Intelligent Beings watch this Earth closely now, ready to communicate? What is the key that will trigger off the unimaginable Powers lying dormant in each of Man? What is the fact, not theory, about other highly-advanced civilisations that existed many thousands of years ago?

Only a man of all times, all places, all ways of life, could answer those questions with authority and certainty. A Being who was present when all those events took place, a Being from outside of this Universe, and yet one who has lived within it.

Just such a Being does exist. Just such a Being relayed the words of Pure Intelligence contained within these pages – through the pen of one who is as you. A Being, to whom no mystery exists, inspired the answers to all of these questions, and many more.

You too, can become a Man Inspired, with a direct link to the Source of all Intelligence – simply. Inspiration is not for the privileged few – Inspiration is for All.